STEIN, WENDY

Atlantis: opposing viewpoints

GREAT MYSTERIES

Atlantis

OPPOSING VIEWPOINTS®

Look for these and other exciting *Great Mysteries: Opposing Viewpoints* books:

Animal Communication *by Jacci Cole*
Atlantis *by Wendy Stein*
The Bermuda Triangle *by Norma Gaffron*
Bigfoot *by Norma Gaffron*
Dinosaurs *by Peter and Connie Roop*
ESP *by Michael Arvey*
Pearl Harbor *by Deborah Bachrach*
Poltergeists *by Peter and Connie Roop*
Pyramids *by Barbara Mitchell*
The Shroud of Turin *by Daniel C. Scavone*
The Solar System *by Peter and Connie Roop*
Witches *by Bryna Stevens*

GREAT MYSTERIES

Atlantis

OPPOSING VIEWPOINTS®

by Wendy Stein

Greenhaven Press, Inc. San Diego, California

Library of Congress Cataloging-in-Publication Data
Stein, Wendy.
Atlantis : opposing viewpoints.
(Great mysteries)
Bibliography: p.
Includes index.
1. Atlantis. I. Title. II. Series: Great mysteries (St. Paul, Minn.)
GN751.S795 1989 398.2'34 88-24470
ISBN 0-89908-056-1

To Colin, Josh, and Jonathan
For your enthusiasm and curiosity

Contents

Introduction

This book is written for the curious—those who want to explore the mysteries that are everywhere. To be human is to be constantly surrounded by wonderment. How do birds fly? Are ghosts real? Can animals and people communicate? Was King Arthur a real person or a myth? Why did Amelia Earhart disappear? Did history really happen the way we think it did? Where did the world come from? Where is it going?

Great Mysteries: Opposing Viewpoints books are intended to offer the reader an opportunity to explore some of the many mysteries that both trouble and intrigue us. For the span of each book, we want the reader to feel that he or she is a scientist investigating the extinction of the dinosaurs, an archaeologist searching for clues to the origin of the great Egyptian pyramids, a psychic detective testing the existence of ESP.

One thing all mysteries have in common is that there is no ready answer. Often there are *many* answers but none on which even the majority of authorities agrees. *Great Mysteries: Opposing Viewpoints* books introduce the intriguing views of the experts, allowing the reader to participate in their explorations, their theories, and their disagreements as they try to explain the mysteries of our world.

But most readers won't want to stop here. These *Great Mysteries: Opposing Viewpoints* aim to stimulate the reader's curiosity. Although truth is often impossible to discover, the search is fascinating. It is up to the reader to examine the evidence, to decide whether the answer is there—or to explore further.

"Penetrating so many secrets, we cease to believe in the unknowable. But there it sits nevertheless, calmly licking its chops."

H.L. Mencken, American essayist

Preface

Did Atlantis Really Exist?

Go to a world globe and randomly choose a place. Chances are, somebody at some time has figured out that the Lost Continent of Atlantis was once located there.

What happened to Atlantis? Did this continent ever really exist? Did it simply drop into the Atlantic or some other ocean? Was a natural disaster such as an earthquake, a volcano, or an asteroid responsible for its disappearance? Is Atlantis fated to rise again from the ocean floor as some psychics have predicted?

Plato, a Greek philosopher, wrote about Atlantis in about 360 BC. His is the only written account of Atlantis remaining from ancient times. But there are other accounts—from psychics who claim to be able to "read" the past. These accounts go into great detail about the Atlanteans, life on the island of Atlantis, and its destruction. There are also, scattered around the world, bits and pieces of physical evidence that *may* be proof of Atlantis's existence.

The possibility that an Atlantean civilization existed and then disappeared 12,000 years ago shatters our current theories about human development and civilization's blossoming. It challenges our beliefs that

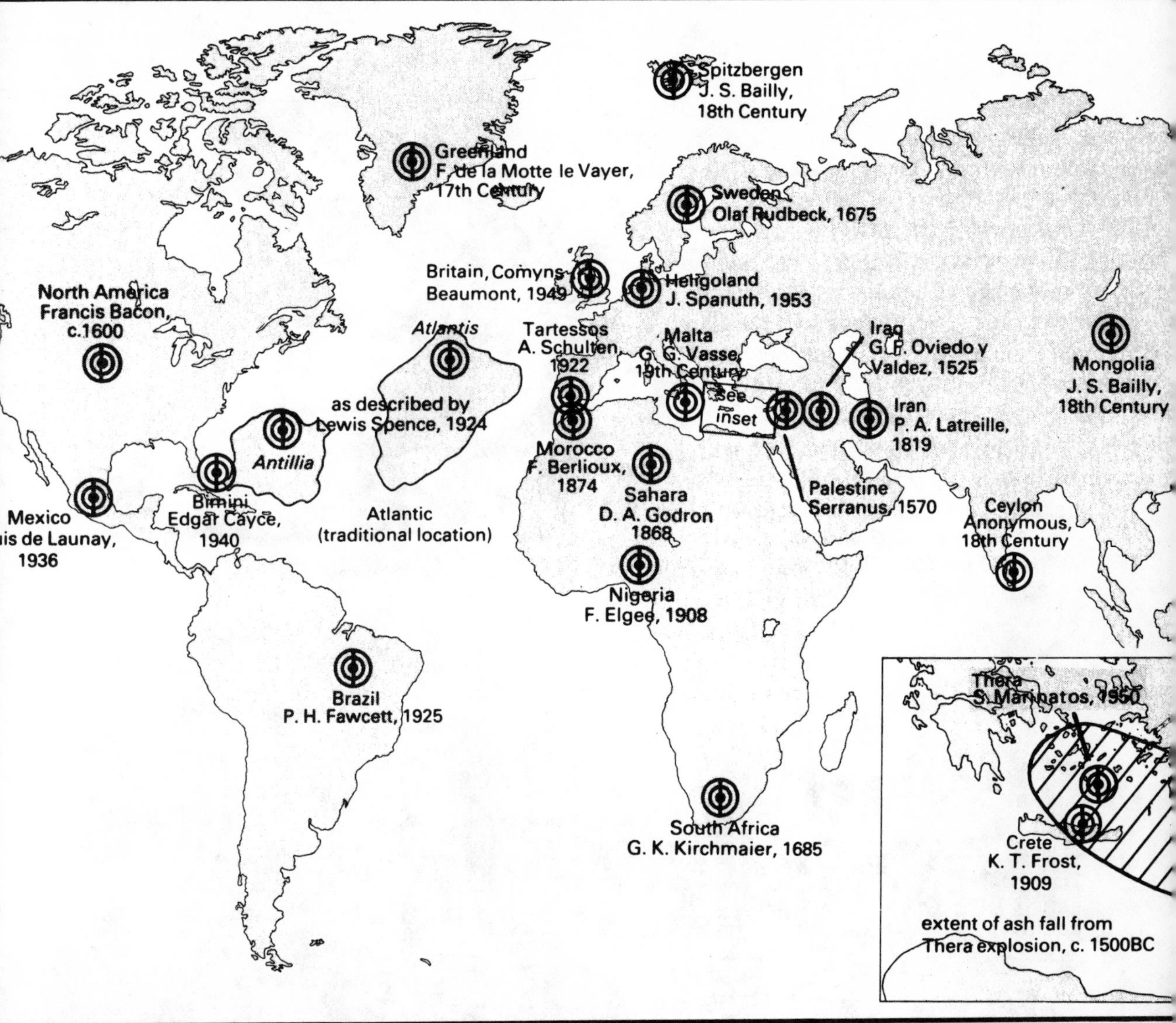

Throughout history, many people have tried to solve the mystery of Atlantis. This map shows many of the locations that have been identified as possible sites of "the Lost Continent." The inset box shows the most popular location in more detail.

Were all of our ancestors simple cave people, or might a sophisticated civilization have existed 10,000 years ago in a place like Atlantis?

people living thousands of years before us were primitive.

Did a highly advanced Atlantean civilization exist long before history was recorded? Is it possible that ancient people were *more* sophisticated than we are? Was their technology so sophisticated we can't even recognize it? If so, what happened to these early people? Did they blow themselves up and disappear without a trace? Have we simply not found the pieces of the puzzle?

The mystery of Atlantis will take us to Greece and Egypt, Crete and Thera, the Atlantic Ocean, and North and South America. It will include the study of ancient civilizations, lost continents, a psychic's predictions, and underwater ruins as well as common myths. We will look at some very unusual ideas about the world thousands of years ago.

One

Plato's Lost Continent

Atlantis, a wondrous and legendary island, is often referred to as the *Lost Continent*. It has intrigued people around the world for centuries.

More than 2,300 years ago, Plato, the Greek philosopher, wrote the oldest known descriptions of Atlantis. Plato lived from about 428 BC to 348 BC in Athens, Greece. About 360 BC, very late in his life, he created two works that are the source of much of our basic information about this fascinating place. These works, *Timaeus* and *Critias*, are two of Plato's dialogues, philosophical works in which he has two or more characters discussing ideas.

Plato and his contemporaries viewed the world's geography differently than we do today. To them, the known world was an island made up of Europe, the Near East, and North Africa. In the center of this island was a large lake—the Mediterranean Sea. The island was surrounded by Oceanus, or *ocean*. A huge continent surrounded the ocean. The ocean and the outer continent were largely unexplored mysteries at this time and for centuries to come.

Plato spoke of Atlantis as a large island situated in the mysterious ocean, to the west of the known

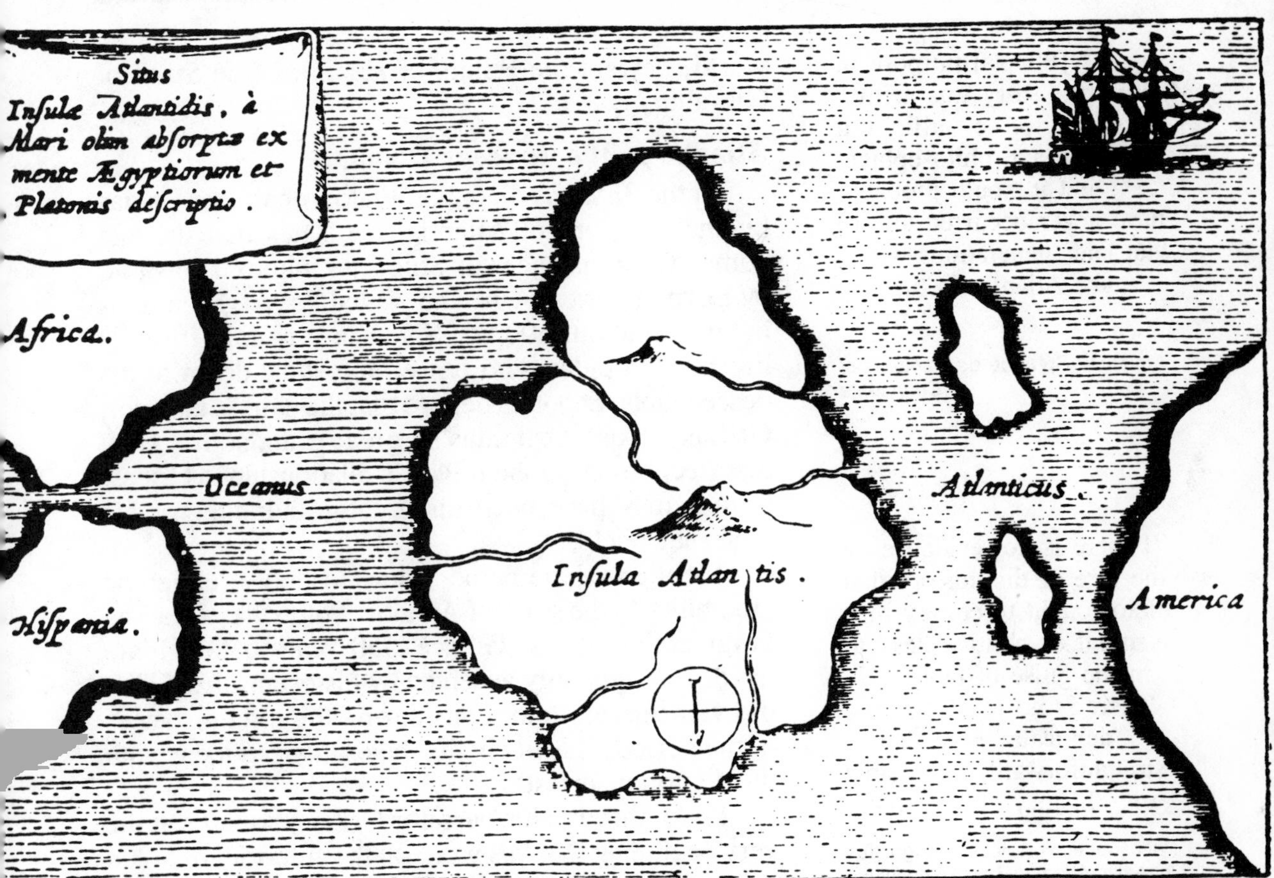

One of the best-known maps showing the supposed location of Atlantis. It is an eighteenth-century Dutch map based on Plato's description. Note that North is at the bottom of this map.

"[Plato's] purpose in writing the story was neither historical nor scientific, but moral and philosophical . . . . and it would probably have never occurred to him that later generations would take Atlantis as literally true."

Author L. Sprague de Camp, *Lost Continents*

"[There is no] evidence on the face of this history that Plato sought to convey in it a moral or political lesson, in the guise of fable. . . . There is no ideal republic delineated here. It is a straightforward, reasonable history of a people."

Philosopher and politician Ignatius Donnelly, *Atlantis: The Antediluvian World*

world, beyond the Pillars of Hercules (the Strait of Gibraltar).

Atlantis in the *Timaeus* Dialogue

In the *Timaeus* dialogue, Plato's character Critias begins the story of Atlantis. He states that the tale comes from his ancestor Solon, to whom it was told by Egyptian priests when he visited Egypt generations before, in about 600 BC. Solon in turn told it to his brother Dropidas who passed the story down to his descendants. Scholars believe that the story's narrator, Critias, was Dropidas's great-grandson. They disagree, however, about Plato's relationship to Critias. Critias may have been his great-grandfather or his maternal uncle.

Mention of the name Solon no doubt lent some credibility to the story of Atlantis. Solon was a leading lawgiver in Athens, Greece, 150 years before Plato lived. It is generally accepted by historians that Solon did visit Egypt. And, considering the circumstances of the period, it is likely that he exchanged ideas with the Egyptian priests.

Plato, through his narrator Critias, stresses at the very beginning that this was "on the authority of Solon to be not a mere legend, but an actual fact." This statement sums up the dispute about Atlantis: Is the story of Atlantis fiction? Or is it an oral history based on actual events?

Critias reports that the Egyptian priests told Solon a tale about events that took place 9,000 years before, or about 9600 BC:

> There was a time, before the great destruction, when Athens was a leader in military power and well governed too. But, there was a mighty power which, unprovoked, invaded all of Europe and Asia. Your great city, Athens, defeated this power.
>
> This mighty power came from an island in the Atlantic Ocean in the days when that ocean was still navigable. The island, Atlantis, was just across from the Pillars of Hercules. It was larger than the

Plato, the Greek philosopher who started the mystery of Atlantis when he told its story in his *Dialogues*.

combined sizes of Libya and Asia. From it, ships could travel to other islands and even to the great continent that surrounds the ocean. For the sea that lies within the pillars, the Mediterranean, is only a harbor with a narrow entrance. Beyond it is the great ocean and the surrounding land, a mighty continent.

Now on this island of Atlantis there was a powerful government that ruled this island, many others, and even parts of the continent. The army of Atlantis had conquered Libya as far as Egypt and Europe as far as central Italy. But it was not satisfied. It tried to conquer Greece, Egypt, and all the territory within the straits.

Greece shone in virtue and in strength. She

stood alone when the others deserted her. She defeated the invaders and saved many from slavery. Generously she freed all who lived within the Pillars of Hercules.

But afterwards, there were violent earthquakes and floods. In one day and one night, all of your troops disappeared into the sea. In the same manner, Atlantis also disappeared into the depths of the ocean. Because of this, the sea in that place can no longer be navigated. It is blocked by mud shallows which the island produced when it sank.

Is this story a fable? Plato is not known as a storyteller, so why would he invent such a tale? Yet, how can it be based on fact? Historians say that the advanced cultures described here could not have existed before 3000 to 4000 BC.

Opposite page: The plan of the city of Atlantis as Plato described it. He visualized a central city surrounded by three rings of water and three of land. Finally, outside the third ring of water, was the Outer City where most of the commercial activity took place. And outside that was the sea. Each ring of land was surrounded by a massive wall, and a canal stretched from the inner city to the ocean. Each ring of land was the site of different kinds of activities. The innermost circle was the place where the royalty, Poseidon's descendants lived. Below: Solon, who supposedly carried the story of Atlantis from Egypt to Greece where it was eventually handed down to Plato.

Atlantis in the *Critias* Dialogue

In the dialogue *Critias*, Critias continues the story about ancient Athens. Then he moves on to a complete description of the foe—Atlantis. He reminds his listeners that he had heard this story when he was a child. It had been handed down within the family from Solon himself.

Critias reported that the ancient gods divided up the earth into sections of different sizes. They made temples and sacrifices for themselves. And Poseidon, god of the sea, received as his share the island of Atlantis. In the center of the island, but looking toward the sea, there was a beautiful and fertile plain. A primitive people lived in this land. Near the plain, and also in the center of the island, there was a mountain where a young woman named Cleito lived. Poseidon fell in love with this mortal woman. He enclosed the land on which she lived by making alternate rings of earth and water around it. He made two rings of land and three of water. He brought warm and cold springs of water to the island. He also made every kind of food grow abundantly.

Cleito and Poseidon had five pairs of male

The Metropolis of Atlantis according to Plato

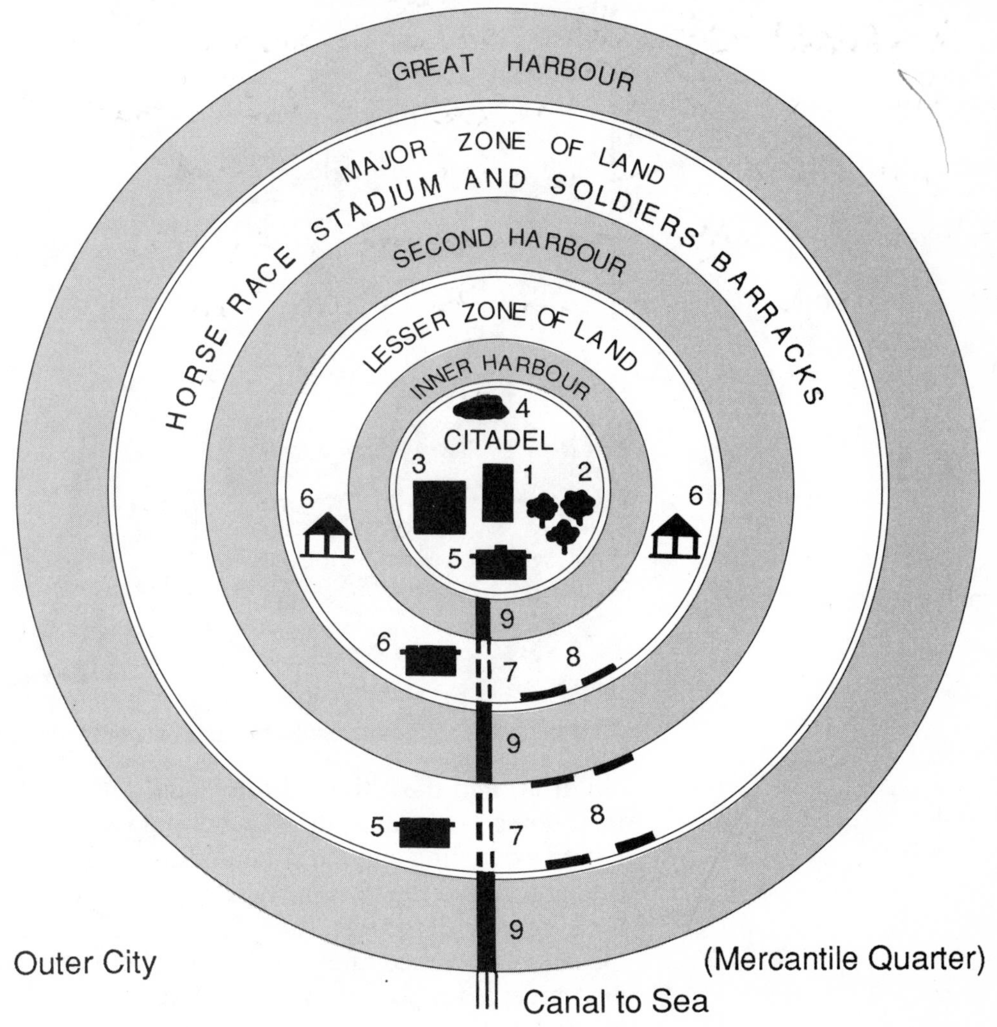

1. Temple of Cleito and Poseidon surrounded by Gold Enclosure
2. Grove of Poseidon
3. Ancient Royal Palace
4. Hot and Cold Springs
5. Guard Houses
6. Gymnasia
7. Underpass for Ships
8. Docks
9. Bridges

Poseidon, god of the sea and supposed founder of Atlantis.

children, and they divided the island into ten parts. Poseidon gave to Atlas, the first-born of the eldest pair, Cleito's dwelling and the surrounding land. This was the largest and the best portion. He also made Atlas the king over all the rest. Both Atlantis and the Atlantic Ocean were named after him. Each of the other sons also received a portion of the island and were made lesser kings, or princes. These sons and their descendants ruled and populated many outlying islands as well.

The Empire

Down through the generations, Critias stated, the rulers of Atlantis had more wealth than any king had

Might ancient Atlantis have been an elaborate and sophisticated city resembling this old temple in southern India?

ever had or is likely to have. Goods were brought to the rulers from all over the world. Animals, flowers, fruits, and vegetables thrived in this land. In fact, the island itself provided everything that was needed, including *orichalcum*, in abundance. (Orichalcum was apparently a metal more precious than gold that was no longer known even by Plato's time.)

Atlantis's rulers built temples, palaces, harbors, and docks. They built a special palace in the same location Poseidon and their ancestors had lived. Each king added to this palace, making it more magnificent than the king before him until it was "a marvel to behold for size and beauty."

The rulers dug a canal from the inner harbor to the outer harbor and then to the sea. The canal was 300 feet wide, 100 feet deep, and about 6 miles long. Even the largest vessel could navigate from the sea

"It is worth noting . . . that there is no mention by any writer before Plato of any sunken island in the Atlantic, and no evidence outside of Plato's word that Solon's unfinished epic ever existed."

Author L. Sprague de Camp, *Lost Continents*

"The evidence presented by the ancient maps appears to suggest the existence in remote times . . . of a true civilization of an advanced kind."

Historian Charles Hapgood, *Maps of the Ancient Sea Gods*

to the outer harbor.

Walls were built around each of the land zones. The outermost wall was covered with brass, the next with tin. The third, which surrounded the inner island, was of orichalcum.

Poseidon's Temple

In the center of the island was a temple dedicated to Cleito and Poseidon. This temple, which was 600 feet long and 300 feet wide, was surrounded by a wall of gold. Yearly, the citizens in each of the ten regions brought the fruits of their lands here as an offering.

All of the temple exterior, except the peaks of the roof, was covered with silver. The peaks were covered with gold. Inside, the temple ceiling was carved ivory. Silver, gold, and orichalcum adorned everything. The walls, pillars, and floor were covered with orichalcum.

Gold statues of the ten kings and their wives were placed throughout. But the grandest gold statue was of Poseidon himself. He drove a chariot pulled by six winged horses. His head reached almost to the ceiling. He was surrounded by 100 Nereids (sea nymphs) riding dolphins. There was also a great altar, magnificent in size and workmanship.

Palaces and Springs

The individual palaces were as splendid as the temple, Critias reported. There were abundant fountains with hot and cold springs. There were baths built for the king and baths for private citizens. There were even baths for the horses and cattle. Some of the water ran off to the Grove of Poseidon, where all kinds of beautiful trees grew in its rich soil.

On the rings of land there were gardens, temples, gymnasiums, and areas for horses to exercise. On the large outer ring, known as the *Major Zone*, there was a racetrack that extended around the island. On each of the three rings of land there was a guardhouse. The most trusted guards lived on the inner island itself.

They guarded the king. Military supplies ready for use filled the harbors and docks.

The Harbor

Enclosing the entire ringed complex was another wall about six miles from the outermost harbor. This densely-populated outer area was the business district. The canal between the sea and the outermost harbor was full of ships; merchants came from all parts of the world. The sound of human voices and the noise of trading went on day and night.

The Plain

To the north, beyond the great outer wall of the outer city was an oblong plain. This flatland was surrounded by mountains that descended to the sea. The plain extended about 3,000 stadia in one direction and 2,000 stadia in the other. (A stadium is about 606 feet, so the plain was about 360 miles by 240 miles.) A great circular ditch surrounded the plain and it caught the water from the mountain streams. The water flowed to the city and then to the sea through the canals. Smaller canals cut into the plain, and the water flowed to the great canal surrounding the plain. With

Hot springs on an Azores island. Plato described such springs as one of the features of Atlantis.

"Time after time the will to believe in an actual Atlantis has been a stronger influence than the best efforts of skeptics to dismiss it as a charming fantasy."

Author Marjorie Braymer, *Atlantis: Biography of a Legend*

"This is all poppycock. There never was an Atlantis."

Scientist and author Isaac Asimov, *The Egyptians*

this network of waterways, the wood and fruit of the island were transported easily to the city.

The Rulers

Critias stated that each of the ten kings ruled his own division and in "his own city had the absolute control of the citizens and, in most cases, of the laws, punishing and slaying whomsoever he would." But the laws of Poseidon governed the kings' relationships with each other. These laws were inscribed on a pillar of orichalcum in the temple of Poseidon. They required the kings to meet after five years, then after six years, then after five years again. (Thus, "they gave honor to the odd and even years.") They gathered to discuss public affairs and pass judgment on any possible violations of the law. But first, they held a religious ritual.

The Sacrifice

According to Critias, bulls roamed freely through the temple. The ten kings, without weapons, but "with staves and nooses," hunted the bulls. When a bull was caught, it was sacrificed so that its blood spilled over the pillar inscribed with the laws. Then the kings prayed and swore to obey Poseidon's laws and to punish anyone who had violated them. When darkness came and the sacrificial fire was cool, the kings put on beautiful blue robes. While sitting on the ground near the embers, they judged any case brought before them. At daybreak, they wrote down their sentences on a golden tablet, and put it away with their robes.

Laws

There were many special laws. Among the most important were those that required loyalty: They must not fight one another, and all must come to the rescue if anyone attempted to overthrow the royal house. They must deliberate together about war and other matters. And, finally, the king did not have the power of life and death over any of his kinsmen, unless the ma-

The great philosophers Plato and Aristotle stroll and discuss life's mysteries—and perhaps Atlantis?

"Deep under the ocean's waters Atlantis is now reposing and only its highest summits are still visible in the shape of the Azores. . . . The great island rose in steep cliffs from the sea. . . . [in] this spot, which after all was clearly indicated by Plato."

Atlantis seeker Kurt Bilau, quoted in *Atlantis: The Eighth Continent*

"Many scientists now believe that no portion of the Atlantic ocean floor can ever have constituted a landmass which became submerged. . . . We must give up the notion of locating Atlantis as a 'lost continent' in the middle of the North Atlantic."

Classicist J.V. Luce, *Lost Atlantis*

jority of the ten kings agreed.

For many generations, said Critias, the people of Atlantis remained obedient to Poseidon's laws. As his descendants, they continued to worship him. They practiced gentleness and wisdom in life and in their interactions with each other. "They despised everything but virtue" and thought that possession of gold and other property was a burden rather than a benefit. They were wise and saw clearly that goodness was increased by virtuous friendship with one another.

But eventually, the people forgot their divine ancestry—human nature got the upper hand. The people grew more interested in amassing wealth than in maintaining their virtue.

Critias reported that Zeus, the ruler of the gods, saw this deterioration of the Atlanteans. He decided to punish them so that they would see the error of their ways and change. Critias said that Zeus called all the gods together and spoke.

—But here Critias's account ended abruptly! We don't know what Zeus said to the gods. Plato left the story hanging. Did he intend to finish the dialogue? Did he simply lose interest? Or was the end of this dialogue lost? We don't know. Nevertheless, we learned many details of the appearance of the Lost Continent.

The Ancient Response to Plato

The controversy about Atlantis seems to have begun soon after Plato's accounts appeared. Plato's most famous student, Aristotle, is reported to have denied the existence of Atlantis. He said Plato made up the island and then made up an earthquake and a flood to destroy his invention. Crantor, a scholar who lived about 335 to 275 BC, accepted Plato's accounts as historical fact. He did not question Plato's descriptions.

Diodorus Siculus, in about 30 BC, wrote that a highly civilized Atlantis was the birthplace of the gods.

Pliny the Elder, writing about 77 BC, mentioned a large land area being destroyed "where the Atlantic Ocean is now—if we believe Plato." Philo Judaeus wrote about a land, such as the island of Atlantis, being swallowed up by the sea.

Ignatius Donnelly's Search for Atlantis

Atlantis appeared over and over in writings throughout the centuries. Many centuries after Plato, the voyages of Columbus and other explorers raised new speculation about Atlantis: Was America the Lost Continent Plato wrote about?

From artifacts like these, found on the island of Thera, scientists can learn much about ancient cultures.

Minnesota statesman Ignatius Donnelly, who revived interest in Atlantis and its impact on civilization.

It was in the late 1800s that Atlantis once again seriously captured people's imaginations. In 1882, Ignatius Donnelly, a former congressman from Minnesota, published *Atlantis: The Antediluvian World*. (Antediluvian means *before the Great Flood*.) Before Donnelly, most works about Atlantis seem to have been based on Plato's accounts. But Donnelly's new work quickly became the foundation for most pro-Atlantean writings. Even today, Donnelly's work is influential.

He set out to prove these points:

- Plato's description is history, not fable.
- Atlantis was the place where civilization first developed.
- Atlantis became a mighty nation, and its people also populated the shores of the Gulf of Mexico, the Mississippi River, the west coast of Europe and Africa, the Baltic, the Black Sea, and the Caspian Sea.
- Atlantis was the original Garden of Eden, where people lived in peace and harmony.
- Egypt was Atlantis's oldest colony.
- Atlantis was swallowed by the ocean, and nearly all its inhabitants perished.
- A few survivors escaped to the East and West. Their stories are the basis for the Flood stories found in the Old Testament, among Native American legends, and in other traditions all over the world.

Critics such as L. Sprague de Camp dismissed Donnelly as a "pseudo-scientist," or *false* scientist. But Donnelly's work ignited interest in Atlantis. Scientists, geographers, explorers, linguists (people who study language), and occultists (people who study and believe in the supernatural) continued the debate.

The Debate Goes On

Geochemist Cesare Emiliani and others have suggested that a sudden rise in sea level, caused by glacial melting about 11,600 years ago, could have flooded Atlantis. (This could also explain the Great Flood stories.) But modern geological theory says that it is not possible for a body of land the size Plato described to have existed in the Atlantic within the past 12,000 years. And certainly, it could not have disappeared without a trace in a day and a night.

Most historians say that the Athens and Atlantis that Plato described could not have existed in 9000 BC. Human civilization at that time was still in the Paleolithic period (the Stone Age). That is, people were still living in caves and hunting for their food. How could such an advanced and organized civilization as that described by Plato have co-existed with cave people?

To us, history began with the invention of writing and written records. Everything that happened before the beginnings of writing (in about 3500 BC) is called *prehistory* because there are no records of the time. Our knowledge about prehistory is mostly theory pieced together from discoveries of ancient bones and artifacts, such as pottery, tools, and ruins found here and there around the world. But prehistory is a jigsaw puzzle with most of the pieces missing. We can only guess what the picture looks like and how the few pieces we have fit. And sometimes, we may even try to force a few pieces together out of frustration!

Writers and scientists continue to speculate about what the world looked like in ancient times. Is it possible that long before our own existed, there was another sophisticated civilization, like that described by Plato, whose records were lost or destroyed?

Two

Was Atlantis the Lost Minoan Empire?

The ruins of a lost civilization have been uncovered on Crete, an island near Greece in the Mediterranean Sea. This Minoan civilization fits much of Plato's description of Atlantis. There are, however, some differences between the dates reported by Plato and those that modern scientists believe are the actual dates of Minoan civilization's existence and destruction. But those who believe that Crete is Atlantis have found a very neat explanation for that: Plato may have unintentionally made mathematical and measurement errors.

Let's take a look at how well Crete fits the Atlantean description.

Crete was the center of the great Minoan empire that flourished for 2,000 years. Its influence covered the entire Mediterranean area. Minoan merchants traveled and traded widely—from Syria, to Sicily, and to Western Europe. K.T. Frost, a classical scholar at Queen's University in Belfast, Ireland, wrote that sea trade between Europe, Asia, and Africa was controlled by Crete.

Little was known about the Minoans until early in the twentieth century when excavations revealed

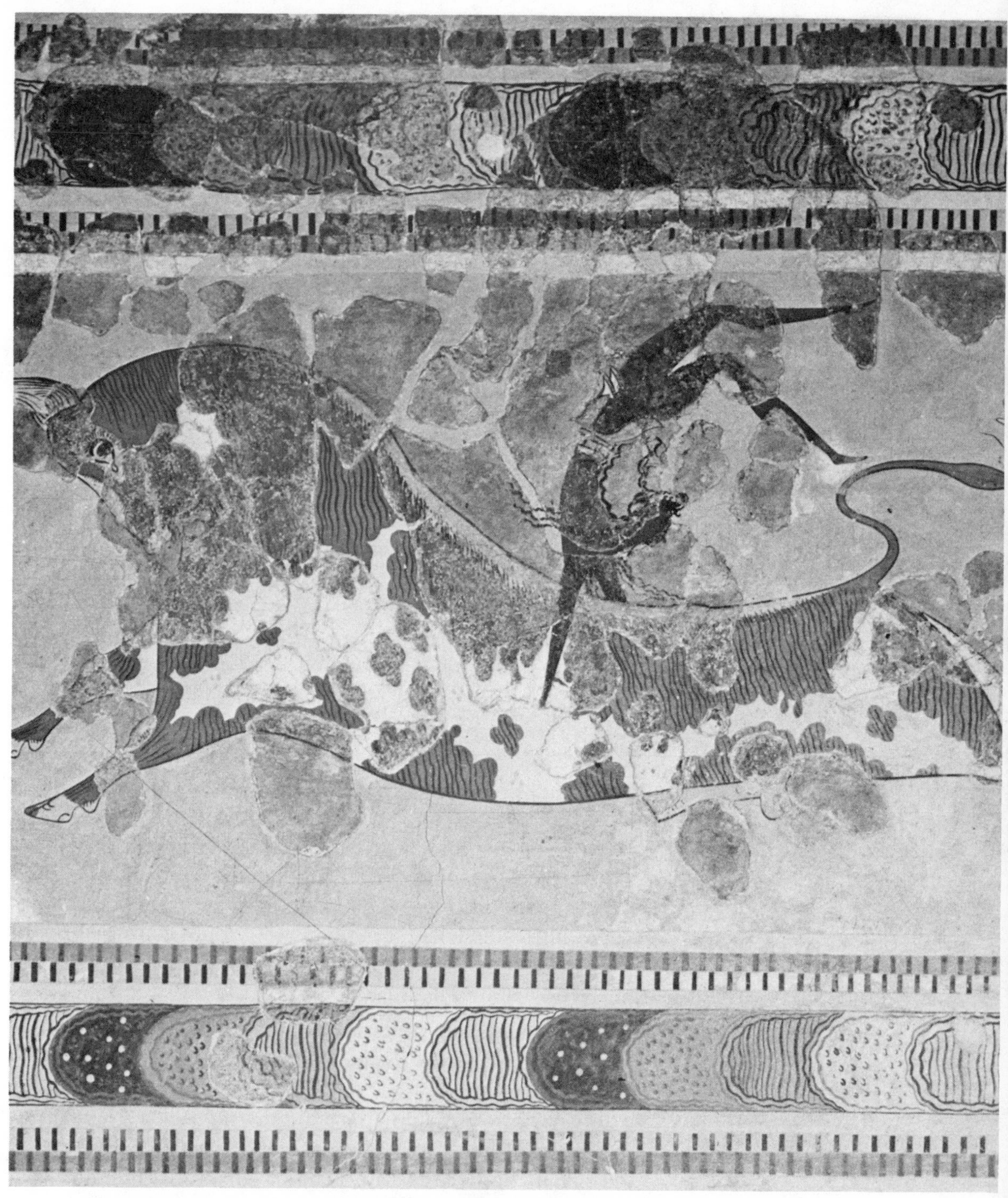

A portion of a famous wall painting from the ancient civilization of Crete. It shows a bull dancer, a youth daringly leaping over the back of a dangerous but sacred bull.

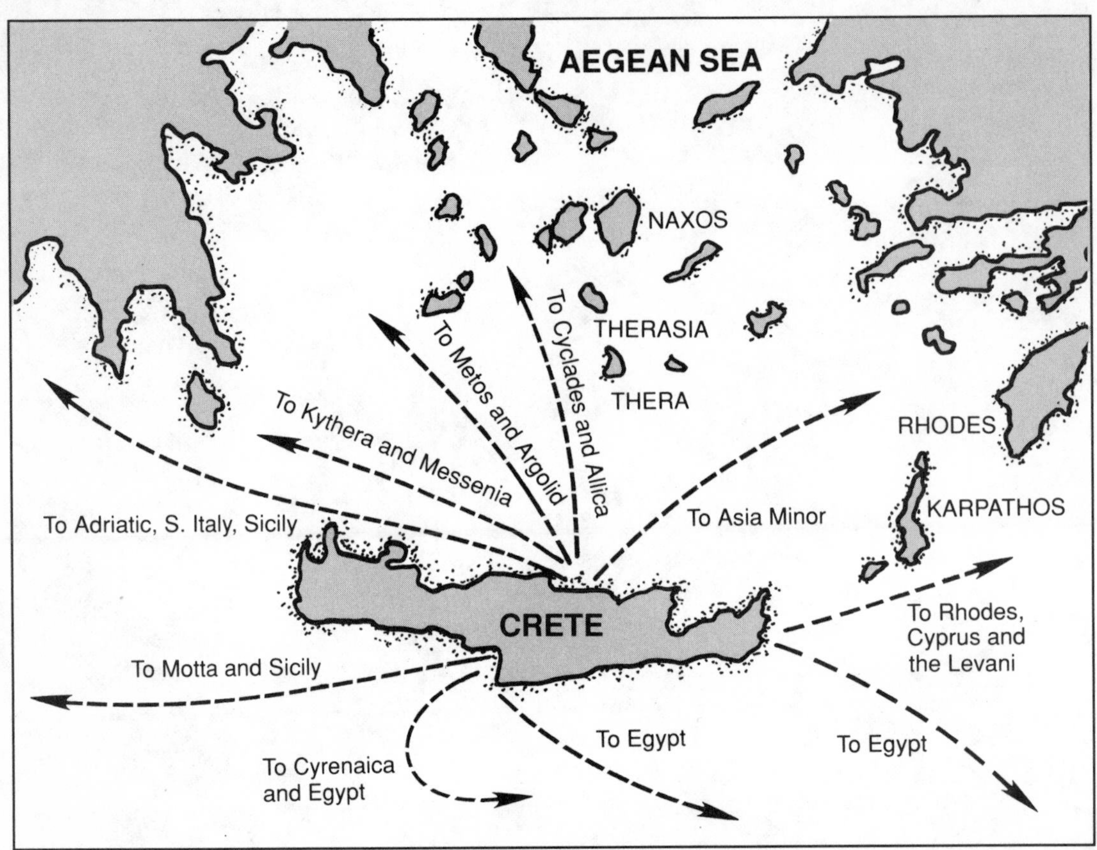

Centuries ago, Crete was a major center of trade. Was it also part of the Lost Continent?

their buildings, pottery, and other artifacts on the islands of Crete and nearby Thera, or Santorini. The Minoans appear to have been wealthy and sophisticated—leaders in fashion, jewelry, artwork, and metalworking. They loved sports, music, and dancing. They had a tradition of bullfighting without weapons. Excavation also revealed that the Minoans had indoor bathrooms with running water.

Excavations at Knossos, Crete

Sir Arthur Evans, an English archaeologist, first began excavating at Knossos, Crete in the early 1900s. Ancient Greek myths had told of Crete's King Minos and his bull-god Minotaur, who was half human and half bull. King Minos had housed this creature in a

A small section of the Minoan palace of Knossos on Crete. Archaeologists are still learning about ancient civilizations from structures such as this.

palace called the *Labyrinth*, a palace constructed with intricated alleyways and blind passages—in other words, a huge maze. Evans' excavations showed that King Minos was no myth. The palace complex was so large and intricate that it could indeed have been a labyrinth. The civilization that Evans unearthed was called *Minoan* in honor of King Minos.

Evans' work revealed considerable information about a previously unknown Bronze Age empire. Other palaces and buildings were also uncovered on the island of Crete. Evans estimated that this advanced civilization had reached its height around 1600 BC. During the next 100 to 150 years, however, something happened to destroy this mighty nation. But what had brought it down? In many of the buildings he unearthed, Evans found evidence of fire. Had the fires been set by humans? Or did some natural disaster cause them? The answer eluded Evans and his associates.

A Daring New Theory

The discovery of Knossos and other archaeological treasures on Crete caused great excitement and in-

"Since Santorin is now conclusively shown to have been Minoan and since the Minoan Empire suffered a catastrophic disaster at the time of the collapse of Santorin, the case for identifying Atlantis with Minoan Crete seems so strong as to be unanswerable."

Seismologist A.G. Galanopoulos, *Atlantis: The Truth Behind the Legend*

"The original story of Atlantis as told by the Egyptian priests can't have been about the destruction of Minoan civilization by a volcano on Thera, because no such thing happened."

Archaeologist Peter James, quoted in *The Mysterious World*

spired a daring new theory. Sites for Atlantis had already been claimed all over the world. But now scholar K.T. Frost suggested a new idea: Crete was the basis for Plato's Atlantis story.

According to Frost, the explanation of Plato's story requires that we examine Atlantis from the Egyptian point of view. After all, the story was handed down to Solon from the Egyptian priests in about 600 BC. Frost asked, what if Plato was simply repeating the description that the Egyptians gave Solon? What if all the geographic information was given from the original Egyptian perspective?

Atlantis's Location

Plato wrote in *Timaeus*, "There was an island situated in front of the straits which you call the Pillars of Hercules. . . . Now in this island of Atlantis there was a great and wonderful empire, which had rule over the whole island and several others, as well as over parts of the continent."

If a ship were sailing *from Egypt*, Frost said, then Crete would be *in front* of the Pillars and the Atlantic would be behind them. Had the seekers of Atlantis been looking in the wrong direction?

According to Frost's theory, Atlanteans would have ruled other islands and continents within the Mediterranean, not in the Atlantic and beyond. After all, the Minoans were said to have ruled far and wide at the peak of their power.

Frost blamed a foreign invasion, an invasion from the Greek city of Mycenae, for the Minoans' downfall and the "disappearance" of Atlantis: When Minoan trading ships disappeared from the seas, it seemed to the Egyptians as if the Minoan empire had been swallowed up by the sea.

According to Frost, there were several reasons for believing that Crete was Atlantis. The description of the harbor and the amount of trade was certainly an accurate portrayal of Minoan activities. He also cited

The island of Crete, thought by some scholars to be the site of ancient Atlantis.

the elaborate bathrooms of the palace and the bull rituals of Crete.

Thera

Decades later, in the 1930s, Spyridon Marinatos, a Greek archaeologist, proposed that it was not Crete but the nearby island of Thera that was Atlantis.

Thera, or Santorini, is an island about sixty miles north of Crete in the Aegean Sea. A powerful volcano destroyed much of the island about 1500 BC. In fact, the volcano sent the center of the island and part of its coastline into the sea. Marinatos theorized that the eruption of Thera's volcano set off floods and earthquakes that destroyed Crete's civilization.

The eruption formed a large caldera, or collapsed area. In his book *Lost Atlantis*, J.V. Luce described the caldera as a giant bay, with "shorn-off cliffs which stand as mute reminders of the volcanic violence to which the island has been subjected. . . . It was as though some gigantic mine had been detonated deep below the centre of the island."

Volcanic Eruptions

The eruption of Thera is believed to have been four times more powerful than the dramatic 1883 erup-

tion of Krakatoa, a small volcanic island in Indonesia. Krakatoa and Thera are volcanoes of the same type. Reports of the Krakatoa eruption can give us an idea of the devastating effects of Thera's eruption.

The Krakatoa eruption was preceded by several years of earthquake activity. These earthquakes even shook Australia. In May 1883, a medium-sized eruption could be heard for 100 miles. The volcano spewed forth pumice, a lightweight, porous volcanic rock, that continued to rain on the island for days to come. Then, in August of that same year, the major eruption filled the skies with volcanic ash. All three volcanic cones were active. The cones collapsed one at a time. When the third and largest one caved in, it took two-thirds of the island's center with it. This caldera is only one-fourth the size of the one on Thera.

The explosions on Krakatoa could be heard thousands of miles away. The air around the globe vibrated. The collapse of the cones sent enormous walls of water crashing against the coasts of Java and

The destructive power of volcanoes is mighty enough to change the landscape and even sink islands. Is this what happened to Atlantis? Opposite page: People flee a geyser of smoke and lava in Costa Rica in 1963. Below: Mt. St. Helens in the state of Washington blows its stack.

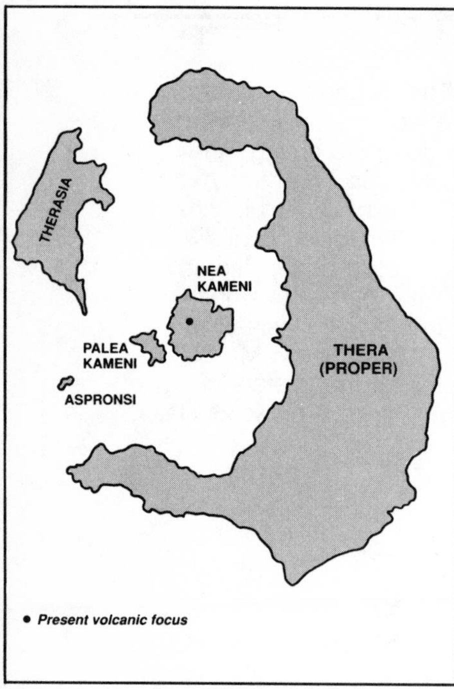

Thera, thought by many to be the true site of Atlantis. Note its shape—the outer islands curved around the volcanic center. Is it possible that at one time this was the central part of the continent of Atlantis?

Sumatra. The waves were estimated to be between 45 and 100 feet high. These massive water attacks, called *tsunami* or *tidal waves*, also sent fires raging through the villages as household lamps overturned and started blazes. (Could this explain the evidence of fire found in the excavations on Crete?) Marinatos believed that the same phenomenon occurred when Thera erupted.

Marinatos studied the eruption of Krakatoa carefully. He was sure that Thera's eruption explained the devastation found under the layers of ash in the excavation at Crete. The eruption of Krakatoa brought down eight square miles of the island. The eruption of Thera brought down thirty-two square miles. Think of the terror that it must have caused, Marinatos observed. In ancient times, surely people must have thought that the gods had turned on them and that the earth was being destroyed.

Tsunami

According to Marinatos, the *tsunami* must have destroyed Crete's fleet of ships and its economy. It also left the island nation undefended. Only Knossos remained, but not in its one-time glory. By 1400 BC, even Knossos was abandoned. The Mycenaeans conquered the island with little resistance from its inhabitants.

A Mathematical Error?

Marinatos's theory sounded plausible, but there remained many unanswered questions. How does the date of the Thera eruption compare to the dates given by Plato for the destruction of Atlantis? Were Crete and Thera too small to be Plato's Atlantis?

Seismologist Angelos Galanopoulos suggested that Thera was part of Plato's Atlantis. He said Thera could have been the fantastic city so carefully described in Plato's *Critias* dialogue. Galanopoulos pointed to the passage in the *Timaeus* dialogue that said that Atlantis "had rule over the whole island and several others." Might Thera have been one of the "several others?''

Galanopoulos based his argument, in part, on his own theory about Plato's math in the *Critias* dialogue. He reasoned that Plato's numbers were ten times too large. Plato had said that the fertile plain was about 2,000 stadia wide by 3,000 stadia long. That was too large an area for the Aegean Sea. But what if you divided by ten? That would leave an island 200 stadia by 300 stadia—a reasonable size for an Aegean island.

This mathematical error would also explain the dating problem. Plato dated Atlantis at 9,000 years before Solon's 600 BC visit to Egypt. Divide 9,000 by ten and that leaves 900. Add 900 years to Solon's 600 BC and you get 1500 BC, the time of Thera's eruption.

Galanopoulos explained the mathematical error by saying that either Solon had made the error, or the Egyptian priests had made the mistake. The Egyptian symbol for 100 may have been confused with that for 1,000.

Galanopoulos reduced all the numbers greater than 1,000 by dividing by 10. That made the size of the

''The whole description of Atlantis which is given in the *Timaeus* and the *Critias* (Plato's writings) has features so thoroughly Minoan that even Plato could not have invented so many unsuspected facts.''

Classicist K.T. Frost, *The London Times*

''While it may be comfortable to take the orthodox line, the chances are that Atlantis actually existed, and that it wasn't Crete.''

Author Francis Hitching, *The Mysterious World*

Part of the ruined Minoan temple of Knossos. Did Atlanteans worship at temples like this one?

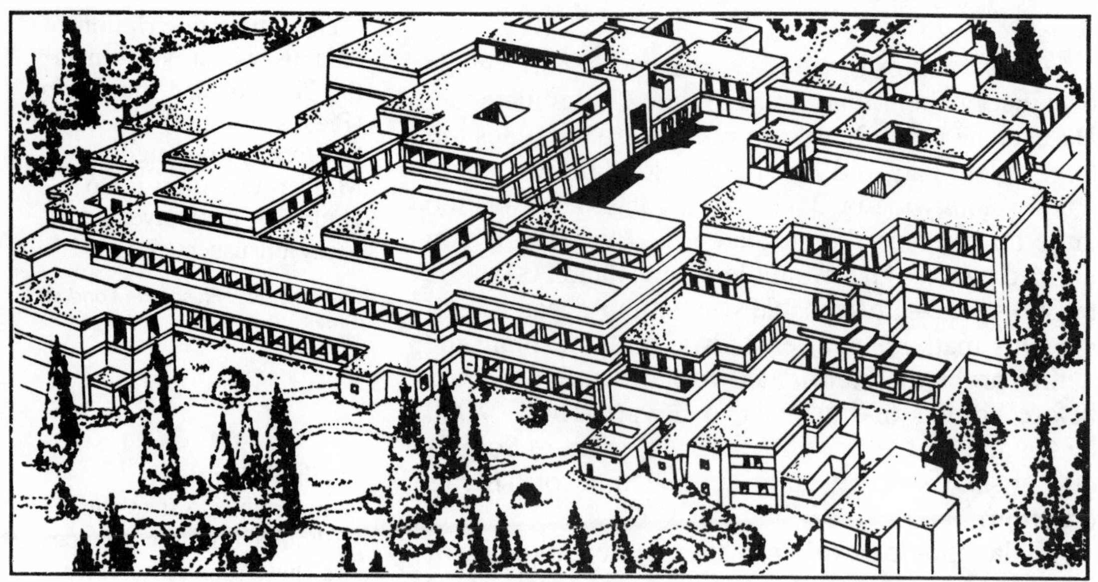

army, which Plato reported as being in the hundreds of thousands, more reasonable too. But Galanopoulos left as accurate the measurements for the city.

Galanopoulos's scale drawings of Thera and Plato's metropolis of Atlantis were almost a perfect fit when one was placed over the other. Galanopoulos also showed that there were traces of canals on the water-covered floor of the caldera.

Marjorie Braymer, in her book, *Atlantis, the Biography of a Legend*, states, "The presence of these channels indicated to Galanopoulos that when Thera was a single round island, there could have been natural rings of land and water in the center. The acropolis [the highest, fortified part of town] would have been the cone itself."

Although Thera was the right size to be Plato's metropolis of Atlantis, there still was the problem of the very large Atlantean plain. Even if the measurements were cut to a tenth of Plato's dimensions, it still would not fit on Thera. Galanopoulos had an explanation for that. Readers had all assumed that the plain was adjacent to (bordering on) the great metropolis.

But Plato did not explicitly say that. The plain around the Royal City could have been on the island of Crete. The Mesara Plain of central Crete fits the scaled-down dimensions suggested by Galanopoulos.

Cultural Proofs

Galanopoulos pointed to other proofs of his theory: Crete had great forests, and it had used its rich resources to build mighty ships. So did Plato's Atlantis. He referred to the red, black, and white rocks of the Theran cliffs and those in Plato's description of Atlantis. He pointed to the great baths and springs of both societies. He pointed out the sacred place of the bull in both Atlantean and Minoan folklore. Wall paintings at Knossos depict the deep blue robes of priests; these robes fit the description given by Plato for the robes worn by the Atlantean kings during the bull rituals.

Galanopoulos and Marinatos and others have done extensive excavation on Crete and Thera. The very fact that there is physical evidence of a civilization makes the Aegean theory of Atlantis an attractive one because there is finally something concrete to look at and study. However, there still has been no evidence that specifically links Thera and Crete and the Mi-

Opposite page: An artist's idea of what the palace of Knossos may have looked like when it was in use. The whole palace complex covered more than 20,000 square meters, or about 3/4 square mile. Below: A wall painting from a Theran temple.

Geologist Dorothy B. Vitaliano, an authority on the volcanic eruptions that may have ended the Minoan empire.

noans with Atlantis.

Critics tend to focus on Galanopoulos's theory about Plato's math. Archaeologist Peter James says there is no good reason to knock a zero off the date, and to divide some numbers by ten but not others. This may make for a nice fit, he says, but there is no reason to believe that Plato made a mathematical error. James points out that Plato made it clear that he was referring to a period of great antiquity—a time longer than 900 years before Solon's visit to Egypt. And there is no reason to believe otherwise. Still, James suggests that Plato's 9,000 years should not be taken too exactly either. He maintains that the ancient civilizations exaggerated their ages to compete with each other.

J.V. Luce agrees. He states that "there is no call to juggle with the figures by knocking off a zero. . . . 9,000 years, I now think, is his [Plato's] round figure way of indicating an 'early' date by Egyptian standards."

Classics professor Edwin S. Ramage also does not think that Thera and Crete were the same place as Atlantis. Plato claimed that Atlantis completely disappeared into the water. But the volcanic eruption of Thera left part of Thera and all of Crete still above water.

Geologist Dorothy Vitaliano does not agree with the Aegean theory of Atlantis for a number of reasons. She argues with Galanopoulos's claim that there are traces of Atlantis's harbors in Thera's waters. The exact physical features of the place before the collapse would have been buried by lava, she claims.

Vitaliano also cites some archaeological problems with the Galanopoulos theory. She claims that the acceptance of this theory would depend heavily on Thera's eruption having occurred close to the time of Crete's destruction. However, she says, there may be a difference of fifty years between Thera's eruption and the demise of the Minoan empire. Peter James also argues that Crete survived the eruption by fifty years or more.

Vitaliano says that natural disaster alone could not have been responsible for the downfall of Crete and the Minoans. But natural disaster may finally have weakened it enough for human invaders to have taken power away from the Minoans on Crete. She insists that if natural disaster was not the sole cause of Crete's destruction, then Crete or Thera could not have been Atlantis.

What Do You Think?

Was Crete the true location of Plato's Atlantis? Did Plato's dialogues contain a mathematical error? Or should we look elsewhere to explore the prehistoric mystery of Atlantis?

"It is . . . quite clear that the story of Atlantis in the original form that we know is not an invention of Plato but an actual story brought from Egypt by Solon."

Seismologist A.G. Galanopoulos, *Atlantis: The Truth Behind the Legend*

"Plato . . . built up a fantasy of Atlantis. . . . Atlantis was never a reality, but the myth was carried on after Plato."

Explorer Jacques Cousteau, quoted in *Lost City of Stone*

Three

Edgar Cayce's Atlantis

Since the nineteenth century, Atlantis has attracted the interest of *psychics*, people who seem to be in touch with a supernatural source of knowledge. This knowledge may come from the spirit world, unusually strong intuition, ESP, or memories of past lives. Although the idea of people having psychic powers is controversial, there *does* seem to be growing evidence that there are people who can "see" the past and even retrieve missing pieces of the prehistoric jigsaw puzzle.

With the 1980s came a new surge of interest in nontraditional spiritualism, and terms like *reincarnation, past lives, karma*, and *channeling* are heard more and more often. Is it possible that we have all lived other lives in other times and places, even on other planets? Can we get in touch with the spirit world?

Although psychics' claims about Atlantis can be neither proven nor disproven without any hard evidence, psychic phenomenon has become more and more accepted as a possibility and even as a probability. If there are true psychics acting as *channels* for spirits—that is, acting as conduits or intermediaries

The Atlantis Edgar Cayce envisioned was a highly developed technological society that may have destroyed itself with its own technology.

Edgar Cayce, the "sleeping prophet," who gave thousands of psychic readings during his lifetime, many of them about Atlantis.

for communication between the spirit world and the physical world—then we do have sources of information about Atlantis besides Plato.

Reincarnation

Edgar Cayce was one of the world's best-known psychics. He gave psychic readings for almost forty years, and many of them referred to Atlantis. Cayce claimed to have access to a body of knowledge called the *Akashic Record*. The Akashic Record is every sound and thought any individual has ever had since time began. Cayce claimed to be able to read the records of the universe; he said he was reading the subconscious minds of people, both living and dead.

Cayce told people about their past *incarnations*—their past lives. The belief that each of us has lived other lifetimes is called *reincarnation*. It is a common belief in Eastern religions. It is the belief that the soul does not die when the body does. Instead, it is reborn in another human form. Problems that have not been worked out in other lifetimes will continue in future lives until they are finally resolved. It is also thought that people we are close to in this lifetime are probably the souls of people we were familiar with in previous lives. Have you ever become friends with someone right away, the first time you met? Perhaps you have a strong connection from past lives together!

Edgar Cayce, the Sleeping Prophet

Edgar Cayce was born in Hopkinsville, Kentucky on March 18, 1877. He was a highly religious Christian man but was not well educated. He left school after the seventh grade in order to work.

As a little boy, Cayce had reported to his parents that he could speak to dead relatives. His parents said he had too active an imagination. It wasn't until he was a young man that his psychic abilities came to public attention.

He developed a gradual paralysis in his throat. No doctor could determine the physical cause. Cayce asked a friend to help him enter a hypnotic sleep. (He often did this as a child in order to memorize his school lessons.) While in the trance, Cayce spoke in a strange voice. The voice suggested a treatment for his ailment. The treatment worked.

Then Cayce learned to hypnotize himself. During trances, he seemed to have a thorough knowledge of medicine. His treatments were very effective. But awake, he knew nothing about the subject. As a religious man, Cayce struggled with the idea that

"Cayce's readings were not mere fantasy, for many of his revelations overlap information archaeology has already collected on the history of the earth. . . . Cayce predicted that ancient records would ultimately be discovered that would resolve the discrepancies between his views and those of orthodox archaeology."

Archaeologist Jeffrey Goodman, *Psychic Archaeology: Time Machine to the Past*

"Cayce's revelations . . . were products of an intensely fertile and overheated imagination, but his 'findings' in archaeology were pure mystifications."

Archaeologist Marshall McKusick, *Archaeology* magazine

some spirit had entered his body. But it did not seem to be evil. To the contrary, it seemed to be sensitive and caring.

News about Cayce's strange powers spread throughout the country. During his lifetime, he did 14,000 life readings, telling in great detail about the past lives of many individuals. So far, no *reasonable* explanation has been found for Cayce's abilities. Many people ask, how could this uneducated man have such knowledge, even in his subconscious—unless he had access to the knowledge of other people or spirits? Or had Cayce himself lived many times before as a healer?

Cayce, the Sleeping Prophet, was soon being asked questions on a wide range of topics. His spirit entity—the personality that spoke during the trances—responded with observations about past lives. It suggested how these former lives affected a person's mental, physical, and emotional health in this life.

Time after time, individuals returned to confirm that information Cayce had given while in a trance was correct. The historical data was researched: His details about other lands and other periods of time proved to be accurate.

Archaeologist and writer Jeffrey Goodman stated that Cayce was either a true psychic or the world's best liar. In decades of doing life readings, his information was never inconsistent. He never contradicted himself. Information given in readings a month, a year, or even ten years apart was consistent.

Cayce on Atlantis

Cayce described an extraordinary history of Atlantis. He presented the Atlanteans as a people advanced in science and technology, but degenerate in ethics. The location Cayce cited for Atlantis was similar to Plato's. In a 1932 reading, published in *Edgar Cayce on Atlantis*, he says: "The position . . . the continent of Atlantis occupied is between the Gulf of Mexico on the one hand and the Mediterranean on the other.'' He added, ''Evidence of this lost civilization is to be found in the Pyrenees, Morocco, British Honduras, Yucatan, and America. There are some protruding portions . . . that must have at one time or another been a portion of this great continent. The British West Indies, or Bahamas, are a portion of same that may be seen in the present.''

But while Plato described the land, Cayce's readings concentrated on the people and their accomplishments. Cayce's Atlantis readings refer to three different periods and three destructions.

The First Age—Human Beginnings

According to Edgar Cayce, spirits existed on earth many millions of years ago. They could enter and leave bodily form at will. Gradually, as they began to enjoy the pleasures of the world, they became trapped, in various physical forms, in the material world. Some of them became human while others became strange creatures, or entities, unknown to us today.

Humanity, said Cayce, took on the physical form that we have today about ten and a half million years ago. Is there any evidence to back up this claim? When Cayce gave that reading in 1925, the idea was considered outrageous. But Cayce's date for the origin of the human race may yet prove accurate. Scientists continue to uncover evidence that shows humanity to be older than previously believed. Fossil findings in the past sixty years have continued to push the history of the human race farther and farther back in time. Current theory says that the first human-like creature existed at least twelve million years ago; our species, *homo sapiens*, appeared 50,000 to 500,000 years ago. Is it only a matter of time before science ''discovers'' that what Cayce reported is true? Is it possible that, while science searches for physical

Archaeologist and author Jeffrey Goodman. He found Edgar Cayce very convincing.

proof, psychics have access to another way of knowing about the past?

Atlantis, the Cradle of Civilization

At any rate, Cayce said that Atlantis was the home of the first civilization. However, as humans became more and more entrenched in their material form, they seemed to forget their divine origins. A rift grew between two groups of humans. Those Cayce called the Children of the Law of One continued to develop and respect the divine, spiritual part of themselves. The others, the Sons of Belial, became greedy, materialistic, and immoral. (Belial was a name for Satan in the New Testament and for *wickedness* in the Old Testament.)

The Sons of Belial mingled and even mated with the strange entities and the animals that lived among them. This mating produced bizarre creatures—"things," as Cayce called them. (If Cayce's visions were true, might these creatures have been the real basis for the classic myths about centaurs, satyrs, minotaurs, and other part-human, part-animal beings?)

After an unknown period of time, the monstrosities and animals that were a result of the corruption of the Sons of Belial became a serious threat to the people of Atlantis and the other continents. Huge birds and large carnivorous animals, possibly dinosaurs, attacked from the skies and on land. Several of Cayce's readings speak of the Atlanteans gathering together with other nations to find a way to rid the continents of the large animals that threatened them all. Cayce said this meeting occurred in 50,722 BC.

By this time, the Atlanteans were advanced technologically. Cayce's readings tell of machines that could speed through the air and through the water. The Atlanteans were also able to harness the forces of nature for energy and communication. They had

Opposite page: Hieronymus Bosch's famous fifteenth-century painting "The Garden of Earthly Delights" showed the artist's vision of earth shortly after its creation. Cayce's descriptions of early Atlantis, with its part-human, part-animal creatures, seems to resemble this artistic vision.

learned how to generate power from crystals. They may even have known how to generate energy from atoms. Armed with their great knowledge, they were able to build explosives to destroy the large animals. One reading spoke of a laser-like death ray.

Remember, Cayce described these things in 1933. Was he talking about the laser and the atomic bomb decades before they were developed by scientists?

It was just such destructive technology that the Atlanteans used to destroy the great animals. These explosions, however, also set off volcanic eruptions that changed the earth's geography. According to Cayce, up to this time, earth had two major land masses—Atlantis and Lemuria, another "lost continent." The explosions caused the southern part of Atlantis to drop into the Sargasso Sea, the shallow, weedy waters surrounding Bermuda. The remains of Atlantis broke into several large islands, and Lemuria began sinking into the sea. One of Cayce's readings even states that the explosions caused the earth to shift on its axis and the North and South Poles to come into their present positions. This first destruction of Atlantis happened close to 50,722 BC.

As a result of this destruction, many Atlanteans migrated to other lands. They carried with them to their new lands the memories of their past place and that ideal time. For this reason, says Cayce, there is some form of a Garden of Eden legend in many areas of the world.

The Second Period—50,000 to 28,000 BC

Cayce's second Atlantean period brought even greater technological development. Communications

Three examples of part-human, part-animal creatures that inhabit mythology. Top: sphinx; middle: centaur; bottom: minotaur. Did creatures like these run wild in Atlantis and later inspire the myths we still read today?

and transportation became more and more sophisticated. Cayce mentioned in a reading on January 23, 1941, that there were machines that "not only sailed in the air but in other elements, also." On September 6, 1928, he described destructive forces, or as he called them, *the nightside of life*. His son, Edgar Evans Cayce, suggests that he was referring to nuclear power.

Cayce also described other Atlantean inventions: elevators, television, radio, and radar devices. Cayce's readings also told of the development of electrical machinery, radiant heating, chemistry, x-rays, and overcoming gravity. He gave detailed explanations of the technology of many of these inventions of the Atlanteans. Much of what Cayce described must have sounded quite farfetched to his listeners in the 1930s, but he might just as well have been describing the present-day United States as the legendary Atlantis of 10,000 to 50,000 years ago.

This second period also was one of great discord over whether to follow the guidance of the Children of the Law of One or the lifestyle of the Sons of Belial. Much of the discord had to do with treatment of the "things" or lower-class beings. According to Edgar Evans Cayce, author of *Edgar Cayce on Atlantis*, the "things" were treated like robots or slaves. The Sons of Belial wanted to continue to use the "things" for

One major theory of the earth's evolution is that in the beginning there was only one continent, Pangaea. Gradually, over many thousands of years, Pangaea broke up, its pieces shifting around the globe until they reached their present positions. Even today, scientists tells us, the continents continue to move.

Did Atlantis have computers as we do today? If so, why was that technology lost for the thousands of years between Atlantis's supposed destruction and the twentieth century?

menial work. The Children of the Law of One wanted to help the "things" reclaim their humanness.

Psychic Power

The Atlanteans had reached a very high level of psychic power. They were able to leave their own bodies through meditation. They understood the spiritual and natural laws of the universe. They were able to harness the power of plants and minerals. They understood the meaning of the stars and their influences.

The Children of the Law of One built temples and, through powers unknown today, were able to treat the "things" by removing their tails, feathers, wings, scales, and claws. With some form of electrical impulse, they were also able to heal their minds.

The Sons of Belial also had psychic powers and knowledge of how to manipulate the natural laws. They used their awesome powers for destructive purposes. There was disagreement over the use of these powers and over the explosive devices and other scientific discoveries. The Sons of Belial used their knowledge for selfish gain while the Children of the Law of One used their knowledge for healing the earth and its inhabitants.

The Second Destruction—The Great Flood

Gradually, as the civilization of Atlantis advanced technologically and materially, Cayce reported that it continued to degenerate spiritually. Lytle Robinson, in *Edgar Cayce's Story of the Origin and Destiny of Man*, writes, "There was a deteriorating of the physical and spiritual bodies, just as there was a wasting away of the mountains and valleys into the sea."

Around 28,000 BC, there was a period of tremendous storms, with volcanic explosions and great flooding. It is not clear whether the Atlanteans and their discord were responsible for this occurrence or if it was a natural disaster. Cayce stated that this was the Great Flood of Noah, described in the Bible.

Some people, perhaps through their psychic powers, knew of the coming destruction. Before this second catastrophe, there was a major Atlantean migration to other lands, especially to the Americas.

The second destruction split Atlantis into smaller islands, with much of its land disappearing into the sea forever. Many people died. Many fled. But eventually, the land quieted down. Order was reestablished among the people. However, the discord soon resumed. The Children of the Law of One and the Sons of Belial continued to battle each other. Scientific achievements were unsurpassed, but the moral base continued to deteriorate.

The Final Destruction—10,000 B.C.

Particularly important to the fate of Atlantis were the Great Crystals or "firestones." The firestones were devices for producing power. The sun's light was concentrated through a reflective stone or crystal which was capped with a special mechanism. The firestones were housed in domed buildings, and a portion of the roof could be rolled back to capture the sun's energy. The crystals could be used to provide power for the cities, to guide aircraft in the dark, and to heal the

"The position the continent Atlantis occupied is between the Gulf of Mexico on the one hand—and the Mediterranean upon the other. Evidence of this lost civilization are to be found in the Pyrenees and Morocco . . . British Honduras, Yucatan and America . . . especially or notably, in Bimini and in the Gulf Stream."

Psychic Edgar Cayce, *Edgar Cayce on Atlantis*

"There is no sunken land mass in the Atlantic; the Atlantic Ocean must have existed in its present form for at least a million years. In fact it is a geophysical impossibility for an Atlantis of Plato's dimensions to have existed in the Atlantic."

Seismologist A.G. Galanopoulos, *Atlantis: The Truth Behind the Legend*

Below: Raw quartz crystals. Could common materials such as this be somehow used in a power machine that could cause a destructive explosion like the one pictured at right?

human body. In the hands of the Sons of Belial, however, the Great Crystals became instruments of torture and punishment.

The conflict between the Children of the Law of One and the Sons of Belial increased. Violence spread across the land. Many people left for safer places. Eventually, the power in the firestones, accidentally turned up too high, brought the final destruction to Atlantis. According to Lytle Robinson, "Gigantic land upheavals shook the foundations of the earth. Great islands crumbled into the sea and were inundated [flooded]. Only scattered mountain peaks remained to mark the sunken graves."

Cayce's Proof

Is that the end of it as far as Cayce was concerned? Must we simply take his word for it? Is there any proof that Atlantis did exist?

Edgar Cayce predicted that there would be some remnants of Atlantis rising out of the water near Bimini in the late 1960s or early 1970s. We'll look at that claim later on. But there may be another surer proof of Altantis.

Cayce's life readings often referred to the historical records of Atlantis. He also repeatedly said that those who left Atlantis took records and knowledge with them. For several hundred years before the final destruction, he stated, large groups of Atlanteans left their homeland for Egypt, Portugal, France, and Spain to the east and the Americas to the west. These people seemed to know that their land was about to be destroyed. They took all manner of written records of Atlantis's advanced civilization with them.

Cayce's readings dealt heavily with the Atlanteans who fled to Egypt. There, the Atlanteans contributed their superior knowledge to help the Egyptians improve their farming, transportation, arts, metalworking, and building. They also helped the Egyptians construct such wonders as the mighty pyramids of Giza.

Psychic Edgar Cayce believed that someday proof of his visions would be found in ancient papers hidden in a House of Records located between the Sphinx and the Great Pyramid at Giza, Egypt.

"While the earliest recorded date in the Cayce readings is ten and a half million years ago . . . civilizations rose and fell many times during the great Atlantean period from 200,000 to 10,700 BC."

Author Lytle Robinson, *Edgar Cayce's Story of the Origin and Destiny of Man*

"Scholars nearly all agree that the earliest civilization of which we have knowledge arose among the Sumerians in Mesopotamia . . . between about 3500 and 3000 BC."

Professor William H. McNeill, *Encyclopedia Americana*

Cayce said that the Atlanteans buried the extensive writings from their home country in a marvelous House of Records, located near the Great Sphinx at Giza. Cayce followers and Atlantists (people who try to prove the existence of Atlantis) hope that the House of Records will soon be discovered. It will prove not only that Atlantis existed but also that Cayce's psychic powers were very real.

Cayce also said that a set of records is buried somewhere in the Yucatan in Mexico, and a third set was buried in the sea with Atlantis itself. Cayce believed that portion of Atlantis would one day rise again. These records would reveal the history of Atlantis and of human beginnings. It would also prove Atlantis's vast knowledge of the universal laws. Unfortunately, none of these records has yet been found.

What Does Cayce's Story of Atlantis Mean to Us?

If Cayce was right about Atlantis, then his words mean our theories about humankind's past are wrong. It means that our modern world is not the first to have reached today's advanced scientific and technological level. It may mean that there have been even more advanced civilizations before ours. But more importantly, if Cayce is right about Atlantis, then his words have an important bearing on the future of the earth. For Cayce warned that there is a lesson in Atlantis's destruction.

The similarities between Atlantis and modern societies, especially the United States, are startling. Cayce's son suggests that the death ray and the Great Crystals could be lasers and atomic power plants. We have made great strides in less than a century. We are perched at the edge: Our discoveries can be used for good, or for destruction. We are constantly making decisions about the moral uses of our new technologies.

Cayce and other psychics say that many souls from lost Atlantis are now reincarnating in the United States and other technologically advanced nations. It is for this very reason that there have been such giant strides in technology—these souls bring that information with them. But they also bring the old spiritual issues with them too. Did they learn from their destruction thousands of years ago? Or are the Sons of Belial and the Children of the Law of One still at war?

Let's Investigate

Like Plato's story, Cayce's version has no hard evidence to back it up. Geologists say no such land mass could have existed in the Atlantic. Historians and anthropologists say civilizations and empires did not exist 10,000 years ago. But our beginnings remain an unsolved mystery. And as you'll see in coming chapters, the Atlantis story just might explain some very puzzling finds that current theories can't explain.

Inside an atomic research plant. Might the Atlanteans have misused the energy from such a facility?

Four

Was Atlantis in the Atlantic Ocean?

Most Atlantis-seekers agree with Edgar Cayce that Atlantis was located in the Atlantic Ocean. They have focused their search there, just west of Portugal. They claim that Atlantis was located there more than 12,000 years ago.

These people seek evidence of an island culture that was highly developed: Its citizens possessed advanced knowledge in science and technology. It was the seat of civilization. They believe that a great catastrophe—perhaps a comet, a meteor, or a nuclear or magnetic device—destroyed it, and the island disappeared into the waters of the Atlantic. Many believe, with Edgar Cayce, that colonists or survivors from Atlantis brought their superior knowledge not only to the Egyptians and other early Middle Eastern cultures, but also to the early peoples of the Americas, for example, the Mayans of Mexico.

The Atlantic Ocean covers 33,420,000 square miles of the earth's surface. Just *where* in this vast ocean was Atlantis?

Atlantists claim that the high mountain peaks of Atlantis may have survived the disastrous flooding. The Azores, Canaries, and Madeiras are all islands

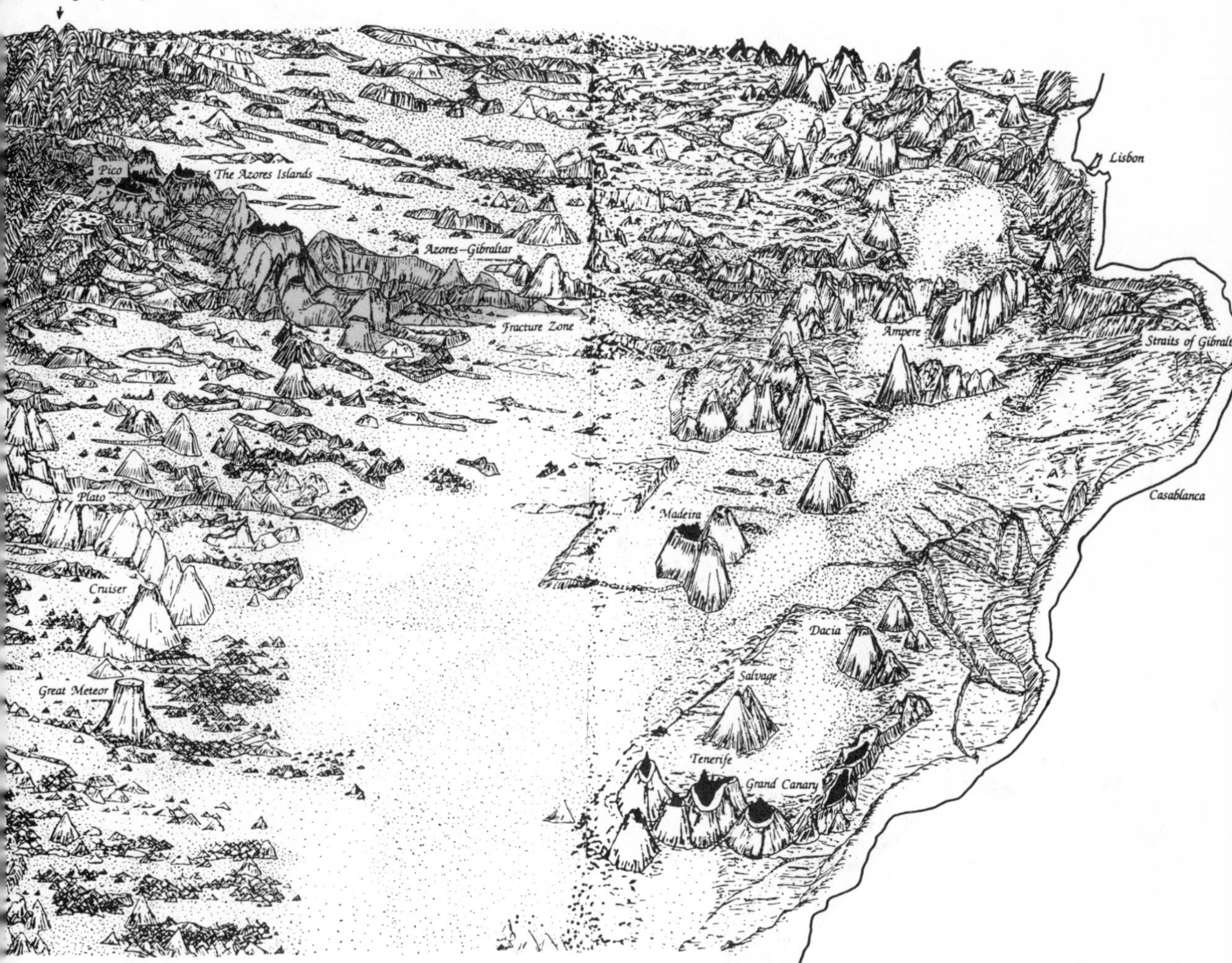

An artist's conception of the ocean floor. The dark points show the land that is above the surface of the ocean. We see these as islands. Some experts think Atlantis may have been located in the tinted area.

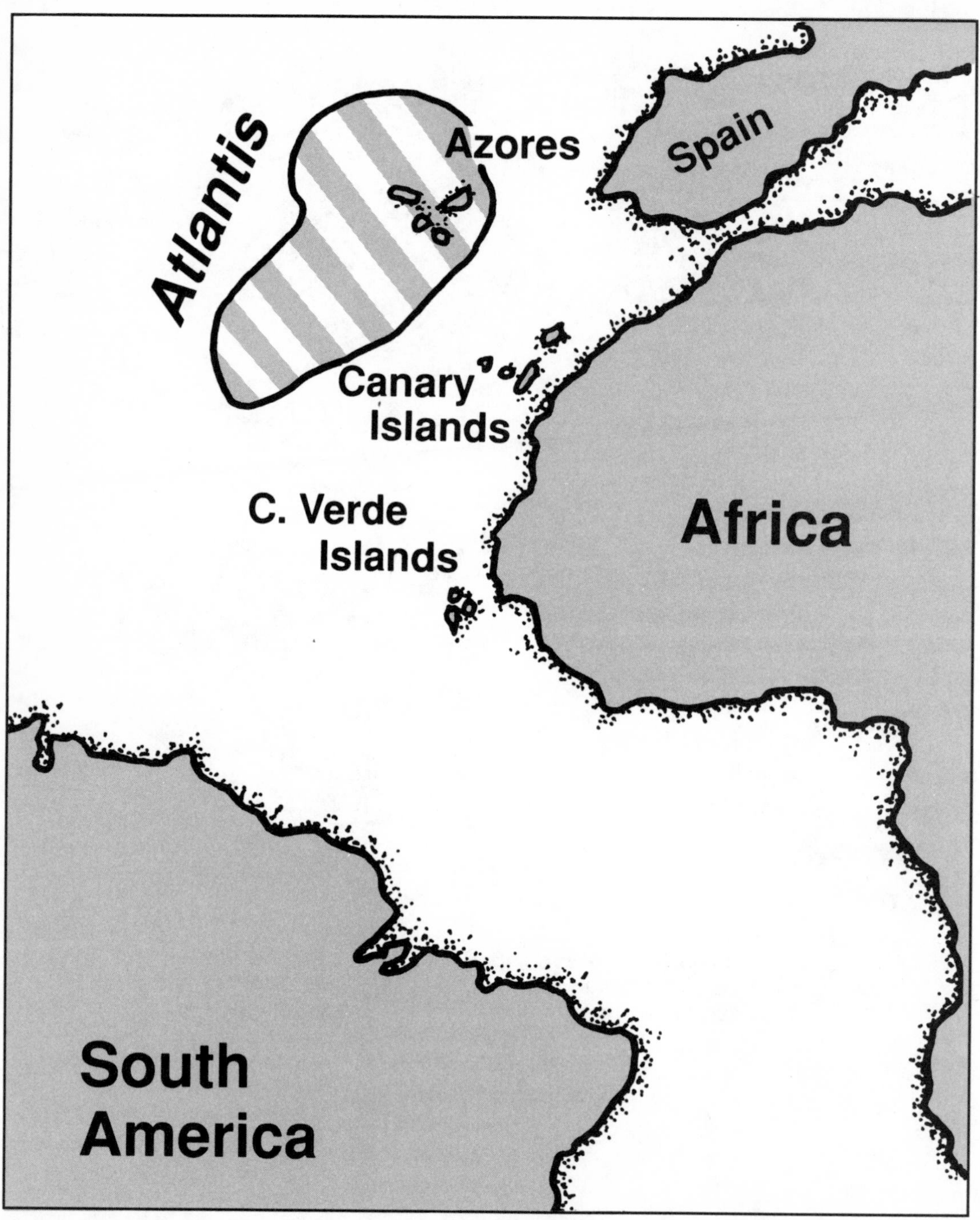

One of the more popular areas thought to be the site of Atlantis. It is located in the vicinity of the Atlantic ridge, a major underwater mountain chain.

off the coast of Africa. The Bahamas are off the North American coast. All of these islands have some claim to being Atlantis's highlands.

The Azores

Atlantis-seekers have focused most of their attention on the Azores. The Azores are nine mountainous islands in the North Atlantic. They are more than 1,000 miles off the coast of Portugal, but almost directly opposite Plato's Pillars of Hercules. They are the peaks of the Mid-Atlantic Ridge, an underwater mountain range that runs north and south along the floor of the Atlantic.

The rocks of the Azores are red, white, and black—as were the rocks of Atlantis described by Plato in the *Critias* dialogue. Plato also wrote that Atlantis had mountains in the north and a great plain in the south. Soundings of the ocean bottom in the vicinity of the Azores match this description. The high peaks of the Azores descend into the ocean, forming lower peaks under the water. Finally, there are both freshwater and hot-water springs bubbling up from the ocean floor in the area of the Azores—just as in Plato's Atlantis.

The Azores are in one of the earth's most active volcanic and earthquake regions. Could that instability account for the catastrophic disappearance of Atlantis?

The Canary Islands and the Madeiras

Just southeast of the Azores are the Canary Islands and the Madeira Islands. The Canaries are a group of volcanic islands in the Atlantic about sixty-five miles off the northwestern coast of Morocco. A few hundred miles north of the Canary Islands lies another mountainous group of islands known as the Madeiras. Both of these island groups are often considered to be part of the Atlantean Empire. They may have been part of mainland Atlantis that broke off during the second destruction described by Cayce, or they may have been outlying islands.

Trident-shaped landmass under the water near Bimini.

> "There is now positive geophysical evidence against the possibility of a sunken continent in mid-Atlantic waters."
>
> Classicist J.V. Luce, *Lost Atlantis*

> "It was clear . . . that if Plato's account was to be treated objectively and all its information utilized, then there was only one region in the North Atlantic where Atlantis might be found—the region of the Azores."
>
> Physicist Otto Muck, *The Secret of Atlantis*

Underwater ruins have been seen off the Canaries and the Azores, but they have not been explored. Skeptics point out that the sea reclaims much coastal land in the course of time, and that the shoreline has been receding for a long time. So it is not surprising that there are underwater ruins off the coast of several continents and islands, including Venezuela, the Mexican Yucatan and other parts of Central America, and the island of Bimini in the Caribbean.

Bimini

On the western side of the Atlantic Ocean, off the coast of Florida, are the Bahama Islands. Some people believe that the Bahamas were a part of the Atlantis mainland, a colony of Atlantis, or an outlying island.

Edgar Cayce predicted that, in the late 1960s, "a portion of the temple of Atlantis" would rise out of the ocean off the coast of Bimini, part of the Bahamas. In 1969, divers discovered stone structures in the waters off the coast of North Bimini. But the controversy continues over whether the structures are natural or of human construction.

In waters about eighteen feet deep, explorers found huge jointed stones. Two sites were discovered—the Road site and the East site. The Road site resembles a huge, reversed letter *J*. Its longer side is about 1,900 feet in length and is made of two parallel rows of large stone blocks. The shorter side is made up of two parallel rows 327 feet long.

The East site has an area of about a hundred acres. A dike with several hundred yards of parallel rows of rectangular shapes borders the south edge. Explorer David Zink and his team speculated that this site was an ancient reservoir. The stones appear to have been underwater for a long time. The edges are rounded and the tops are "domed" like "giant loaves of bread or pillows of stone."

These stones are a natural construction, geologists argue. Beach rock erosion and cracking can form very

Note the pattern of these stones found near Bimini. They appear to have been put together purposefully. Might they have been part of an Atlantean city?

regular blocks of rock. But Zink writes, in *The Stones of Atlantis*, that the joints between the stones in the Road site are "so narrow, they resembled masonry."

Zink's team turned up even more puzzling finds. There were three stones, which together narrowed to an arrow pointing east. They seemed to point to two long, thin cylindrical stones that looked "very much like obelisks" although they were lying on their sides instead of standing upright. (Obelisks are tall, four-sided pillars that come to a point at the top.) This setup seemed to be a "layout oriented to the equinox," writes Zink.

The Zink team also found an ancient block with a tongue-and-groove pattern. It proved to be undatable. It is impossible to determine whether it came from a passing ship, or was carried underwater from far away by the current, or is truly a relic from a lost civilization near Bimini.

The Geological Testimony for Atlantis

Geologists say that millions of years ago there was only one continent which they call *Pangaea*. It was surrounded by water. Slowly, however, that continent broke up into two continents called *Laurasia* and *Gondwanaland*. These two continents slowly moved apart until there were the seven continents we have

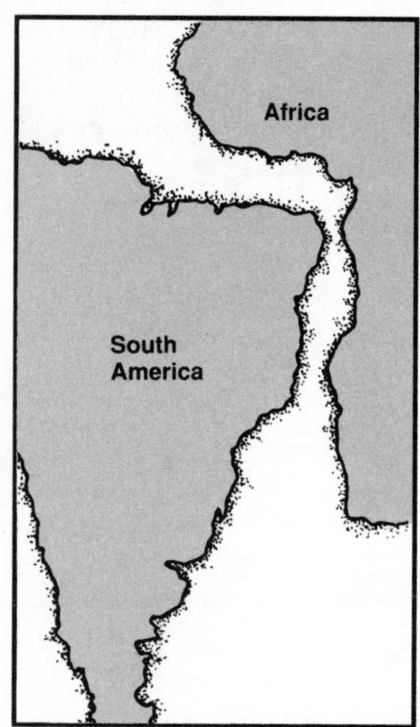

If moved together, the continents of South America and Africa would fit together almost like the pieces of a jigsaw puzzle.

today. Was Atlantis once the eighth?

If you cut out the continents from a map and pieced them together, you would see that the continents fit together fairly neatly, like a jigsaw puzzle. Writer and researcher Charles Berlitz says that all the pieces fit togther with scarcely a missing piece *except* in the southern section of the North Atlantic. That is the area outside Plato's Pillars of Hercules.

Active and Unstable Area

The Mid-Atlantic is considered to be a very active and unstable geological area. Three major tectonic plates meet near the Azores. (Tectonic plates are the underlying structural plates of the earth's crust.) The movement of the plates causes volcanic eruptions and earthquakes. It might also create new land masses and then cause them to be swallowed up. Berlitz, in *Atlantis, the Eighth Continent*, presents many accounts of islands that appeared and then disappeared in the Atlantic. Ship crews reported seeing uncharted islands that weeks later were no longer visible. Both ship and airplane crews have reported seeing underwater ruins.

Author Francis Hitching points out in his book, *The Mysterious World: An Atlas of the Unexplained*, that geology is a theoretical science. That is, it is based on logical conclusions drawn from an incomplete set of facts. There is no concrete proof that these conclusions are correct.

Atlantis does not fit current theories concerning the formation and disappearance of land masses. But knowledge changes, and perhaps tomorrow the mystery of Atlantis will yield to a new theory.

Geologists and Atlantis

Most geologists say that there could not have been a large land mass in the Atlantic within the past 12,000 years. If there ever was another continent or large island, it existed before humans inhabited the planet.

The Azores could not be the remnants of an ancient island, they say, because the Mid-Atlantic Ridge is a new structure, not an old one that is sinking.

Geologist Dorothy Vitaliano says that the Mid-Atlantic Ridge is "one of the youngest large-scale features on the face of the earth. It is being built up on the ocean floor of new material erupted from deep in the earth's mantle along a vast rift along its center." If the Mid-Atlantic Ridge is in its building stage, then it would be impossible that a large land mass has sunk there. The ridge is still growing, not sinking, says Vitaliano. Furthermore, the material of the earth's crust underneath the continents is different than that under the ocean floor. And there is no sign on the ocean floor of any crust that could have been a continent.

Vitaliano also dismisses a favorite story told by Atlantis enthusiasts: In 1898, a crew was laying a trans-Atlantic cable. The cable broke about 500 miles north of the Azores. Fortunately, the crew was able to bring up the cable. They also brought up chips of rock from a depth of more than 10,000 feet. A geologist identified the chips as *tachylite*, a black, glassy volcanic rock, created when molten lava cools. Tachylite supposedly forms above water, not beneath it. And it would supposedly disintegrate in seawater—especially after 15,000 years. Those convinced of the existence of Atlantis conclude, then, that the Azores must have been part of a larger land mass existing above water within the last 15,000 years. Vitaliano says, however, that tachylite has been known to form in water as deep as 17,000 feet. Cold seawater would harden the molten lava as effectively as would cool air.

Vitaliano does not completely dismiss the notion that islands can rise and sink. But they do so gradually, she says. They do not disappear in a day and a night, as Plato claimed.

Skeptics also add that much of the Atlantic Ocean floor has been explored without finding any hint of

"It is safe to say that no continent with a high civilization . . . existed in the Atlantic 10,000 years ago, because it would have left relics of that age on the neighboring shores of North America, Europe, and Africa, which it did not."

Author L. Sprague de Camp, *Lost Continents*

"A common objection to the theory of a prehistoric civilization is contained in the following question: If there were an extensive civilization of such great antiquity, why have no cultural artifacts been found? One answer would be that any artifacts remaining from a period so far back in time would no longer be easily recognizable or would have disappeared through disintegration or rust."

Author Charles Berlitz, *Atlantis, the Eighth Continent*

Stone wall carvings from four different cultures that show surprising similarities. From left to right: Mayan, Egyptian, Indian, Babylonian. Were the similarities in these cultures due to the influence of common ancestors —Atlanteans?

a submerged island nation. But think how difficult it was to locate the sunken ship, *Titanic*. It had been submerged for only a few decades, and searchers even had an idea of where to look. Yet finding the wreck was like finding a needle in a wet haystack!

Descendants of Atlantis

Geologists say no to an Atlantis. But if there was no Atlantis, why do so many peoples who live along the North Atlantic have similar names for an island or continent that once supposedly existed there?

The Basques live in northern Spain and western France. Yet their language is distinct from the other peoples of those nations. In fact, they are sometimes called the descendants of Atlantis because their origins are undetermined. They call Atlantis *Atlaintika*. The inhabitants of the Canary Islands also claim kinship with Atlantis. Their name for the missing island is *Atalaya*.

Other ancient peoples also believed there was such an island in the Atlantic. The Vikings called it *Atli*.

The Phoenicians called it *Antilla*. The ancient Egyptians wrote of a land called *Amenti*, and the Babylonians called their primordial paradise *Arallu*. The Aztecs of Mexico believed they came from an island to their east called *Astlan*. Throughout Mexico there are other place names that also sound much like the name Atlantis—*Azatlan* and *Atlan*, for example.

The Hopi and some other Native American tribes have traditions that tell of their ancestors' homeland: an island in the Atlantic. The Mayans, Toltecs, and other Central American peoples have legends that trace their ancestry to an island to the east. Even in India there is a reference to a place called *Attala*.

So many diverse peoples have similar names for this missing land. Could this mean that there is some basis for the legend of Atlantis?

Ancient Maps

People who believe Atlantis really existed thousands of years ago look to an additional source of evidence to support their belief: Several ancient

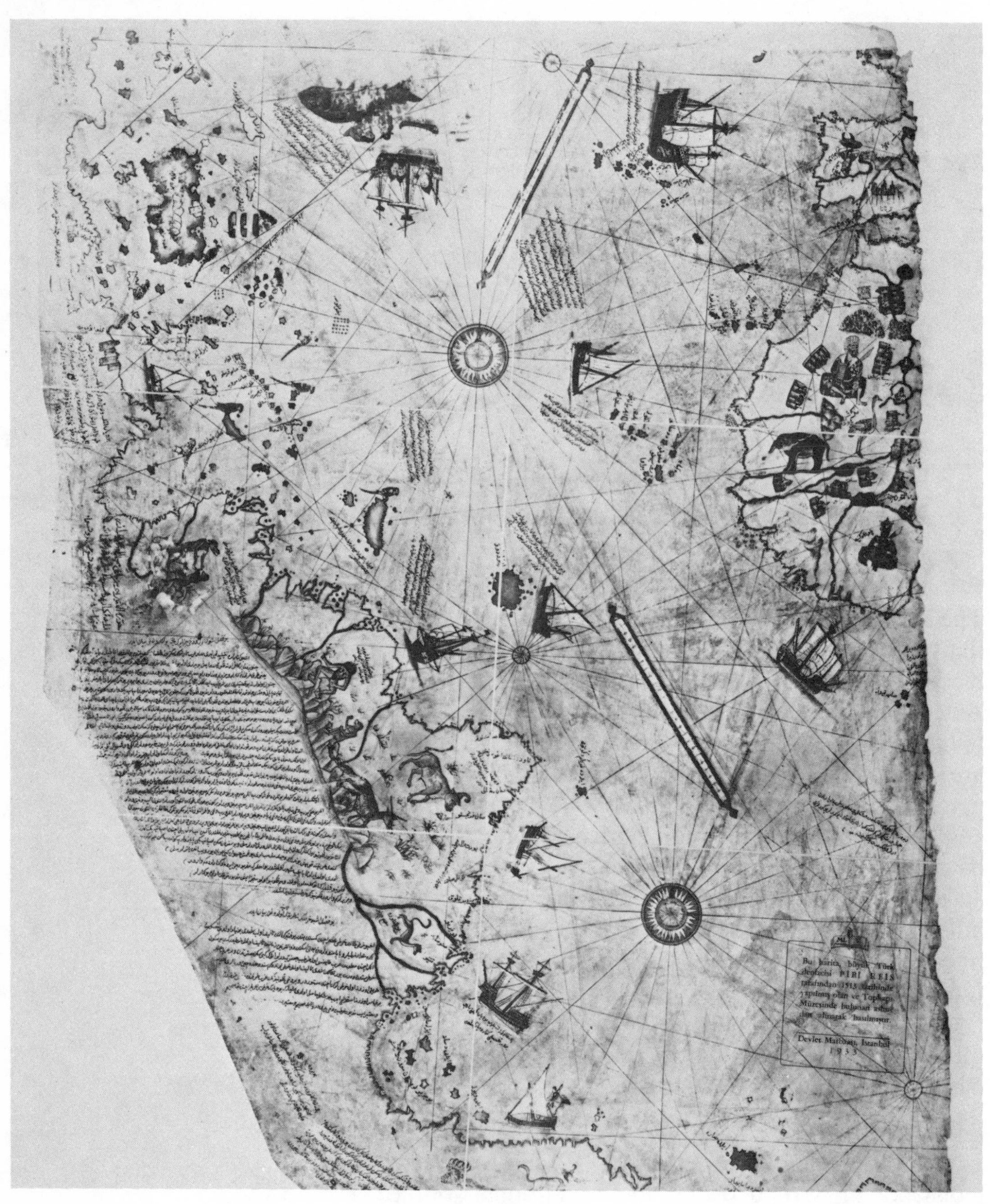

The Piri Re'is map.

maps have been found that have accurate outlines of the Americas long before Christopher Columbus's famous voyage to the New World. The maps also show Antarctica before its "discovery" in the 1800s. The most famous is the Piri Re'is map. It not only shows Antarctica before it was covered with ice, but also a large island in the Atlantic.

Piri Re'is was a Turkish admiral who lived in the sixteenth century. The map was discovered in Istanbul in 1929. In a note written on the map, Re'is said he had used maps and charts from the time of Alexander the Great (356-323 BC) to draw this map. Those maps were probably copies of earlier maps from Egypt which in turn were copies of still earlier maps, from before the time when ice covered Antarctica. Those original maps were probably housed in the ancient library in Alexandria along with almost one million other documents. The administrators of the library had collected copies of every document they knew about in the world. Most of the documents were lost to fire during the time of Julius Caesar (100-44 BC) and another later fire.

Science historian Charles Hapgood, and other scientists, suggest that documents concerning Atlantis may have been among the lost collection. That is why there is no reference to Atlantis other than in Plato's writings.

Hapgood has thoroughly studied the Piri Re'is map and other ancient maps. In his book, *Maps of the Ancient Sea Kings*, he comes very close to actually claiming that the huge Atlantic island on the Piri Re'is map could be Atlantis. He writes that on some reproductions of the map, there is a deep shade of color around the coastline of this island, and that this seems to suggest that highlands or mountains surrounded an interior plain. This would agree with Plato's description of Atlantis. Hapgood also points out that the harbors on the map are carefully detailed.

He notes that the island is right over the under-

"There is this to be said for any lost continent: It is as difficult to make a case for its previous existence as to prove that it never existed."

Author Marjorie Braymer, *The Making of a Legend*

"Hitherto, people have not seriously believed that an advanced civilization could have preceded the civilization now known to us. The evidence, therefore, has been neglected."

Historian Charles Hapgood, *Maps of the Ancient Sea Gods*

water Mid-Atlantic Ridge, and that other ancient maps also testify to the existence of an island in this same location near the equator.

Hapgood also refers to the findings of a Belgian scientist, Dr. René Malaise, who concluded that parts of the Mid-Atlantic Ridge were still above water at the end of the Ice Age. Malaise studied sediment from the top of the ridge. In the sediment, he found freshwater diatoms (microscopic algae). They must have lived in a freshwater lake when the ridge was above water. The species of diatoms were all geologically recent, which meant that the freshwater lake existed in the past 10,000 to 15,000 years.

According to most scientists, people who lived 10,000 or more years ago were in the Stone Age. It would be impossible for anyone to have mapped the world or even to have explored it. Who then drew the maps of this ancient world? How were they able to make such accurate maps of the world, including Antarctica?

Some pro-Atlantists say that the Piri Re'is map does more than show that ancient people knew about Atlantis. They believe that the Atlanteans made the

Did all of our ancestors of several thousand years ago use tools as primitive as the hammer on the left or might some people—Atlanteans?—have had sophisticated instruments such as this thousand-year-old astrolabe, used to determine the positions of the stars?

original map that was stored in the library at Alexandria. Charles Hapgood writes, "This island, if it really existed, would have been ideally suited by climate and location for agricultural and commercial development. An ideal home for a sea people! A secure base for a maritime empire whose ships would have had easy access to commercial ports in the Caribbean, South America, Europe, in Africa, even perhaps in Antarctica. *Here, in this island, there might have developed the people who made these maps*."

Atlantis supporters also suggest that the Atlanteans, with their advanced technology, were able to survey the continents from the air or even from space. Hapgood believes that the Piri Re'is map and other ancient maps point to an advanced world existing before the civilizations we know about. As to why there is no evidence of this, Hapgood says, "The more advanced the culture, the more easily it will be destroyed, and the less evidence will remain."

If highly advanced civilizations did exist, why do only stone implements and structures remain? Stone does not disintegrate as quickly as do metals and other materials. It is unlikely that metal tools from 12,000

San Francisco, California, before and after its infamous earthquake of 1906. Did a natural destructive force such as this destroy Atlantis and send it deep into the sea?

or more years ago would remain to this day. Will our civilization appear to have been a Stone Age 10,000 years from now?

When Did Atlantis Exist?

Most archaeologists say that a civilization like the one Plato describes could not have existed before 4000 to 3000 BC. And a civilization such as the one that Cayce describes could not have existed until today!

According to the most accepted chronology (sequence of events) of prehistory, in 10,000 to 9000 BC, human civilization was still in the Stone Age. People had not yet learned to work with metals. They were still using primitive stone implements. In 9000 BC, six hundred years *after* Plato's date for the destruction of Atlantis, people were just beginning to learn how to farm and to domesticate animals. It wasn't until 6000 BC that there were small, permanent farming communities. And it wasn't until 3500 BC that these began to reach the size of small cities. At about that time, people also started making bronze tools and weapons. The wheel was finally invented about 3000 BC, which then led to the development of the cart, wagon, and chariot.

How could a place like Plato's Atlantis have existed more than 12,000 years ago? Here was a well-developed society with laws, palaces, trade, metal tools and weapons, war chariots, ships, art, religion, running water, fine clothing, and writing. The existence of Edgar Cayce's Atlantis would be even more farfetched, with its flying machines, radar, medical technology, and super-energy sources.

There are several explanations for these differing accounts of prehistory:

- It is very possible that Atlantis didn't exist. Acceptance of that finding would leave our whole view of the world and its development intact. We would not have to revise any of our accepted theories.
- The dates given for Atlantis are too early. Atlantis did not exist until a long time after 9600 BC. Atlantis may really have been the islands of Crete and Santorini. They were partially destroyed *900* years, not 9,000 years before Solon's trip to Egypt.
- Atlantis existed as a highly advanced civilization in the midst of a very primitive prehistoric world.
- Atlantis was part of a very advanced world that was destroyed.

"The very best we can do is grant that Plato might have derived some of his ideas from Minoan Crete in one way or another, but . . . from the geological point of view I fear that Atlantis must be considered just another of the myths of Plato."

Geologist Dorothy Vitaliano, in *Atlantis: Fact or Fiction*

Prehistoric Scientists

Did an advanced civilization such as Atlantis exist 12,000 years ago? Are we simply relearning the skills and technology that other civilizations had invented?

Science historian Charles Hapgood speculated that there were mapmakers before 10,000 BC. They had instruments for measuring latitude and longitude. He

"If Plato had sought to draw from his imagination [only] a wonderful and pleasing story, we should not have had so plain and reasonable a narrative. . . . It is a singular confirmation of his story that hot springs abound in the Azores, which are the surviving fragments of Atlantis."

Ignatius Donnelly, *Atlantis, the Antediluvian World*

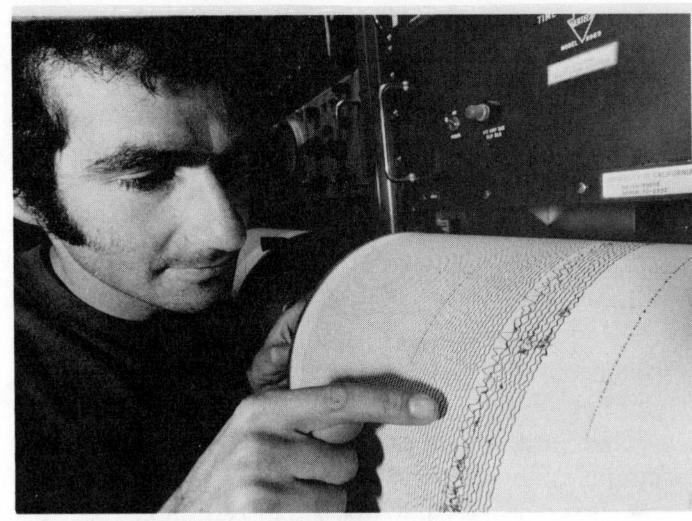

A scientist examines earthquake reading on a seismograph.

also says that these people were experts in measuring the earth and other celestial bodies.

Rock crystal magnifying lenses have been found in Asia Minor and Crete. The ancient Chinese worked with aluminum. They also recorded earthquakes with seismographs (instruments for measuring vibrations within the earth). Their records are helping today's scientists predict major earthquakes.

A wall painting in a temple in Egypt shows two priests carrying objects that look like light bulbs. The bulbs seem to be resting on insulators and are hooked up to a large braided cable.

Objects that resemble today's batteries have been found in an area near the Caspian Sea.

An ancient model of the solar system was recovered from the sea off the shores of Greece. It seems to be a kind of computer based on the stars. One scientist observed, "Finding this device is like finding a jet plane in the tomb of King Tut."

Many archaeologists say that museums around the world own artifacts, presently locked away, that would shake up our current understanding of the prehistoric world. But, say those archaeologists, conventional science is reluctant to reconsider and revise that understanding even in the light of new data—especially if those data don't fit accepted theories.

But as you will soon read, Atlanteans and other ancient peoples may have had very accurate skills in astronomy, mathematics, building, and measurement.

"The arguments of most members of the Atlantist cult are not to be taken very seriously."

Author L. Sprague de Camp, *Lost Continents*

"Some scholars . . . have dedicated years of their lives in an attempt to prove that the study of Atlantis is a waste of time."

Author Charles Berlitz, *Atlantis, the Eighth Continent*

Five

The Legacy of Atlantis

The Atlantis controvery does not end with the disappearance of Atlantis into the ocean. The island nation, if it existed, was swallowed up with most of its inhabitants. But some Atlanteans may have fled and taken their culture, inventions, and knowledge to many parts of the world. As we have seen, many countries and cultures have strong similarities in some of their legends and place names. There are also many cultural similarities. To some, these are the most convincing evidence of all that Atlantis was a real place.

Archaeologists and anthropologists disagree about how culture and civilization spread throughout the world. Were inventions such as the wheel, writing, calendars, and so on developed independently in various parts of the world? Or were they developed in one place and spread through trade and travel?

There is growing evidence that there was contact across the Atlantic Ocean before 4000 BC. There is also evidence that, according to some interpretations, may be proof that the Atlanteans migrated to Egypt and the Americas. For example, cultures on both sides of the Atlantic Ocean share common traits. They also share similar architectural remains: Pyramids,

Mayan ruins on the edge of the ocean. Was this culture influenced by Atlantis?

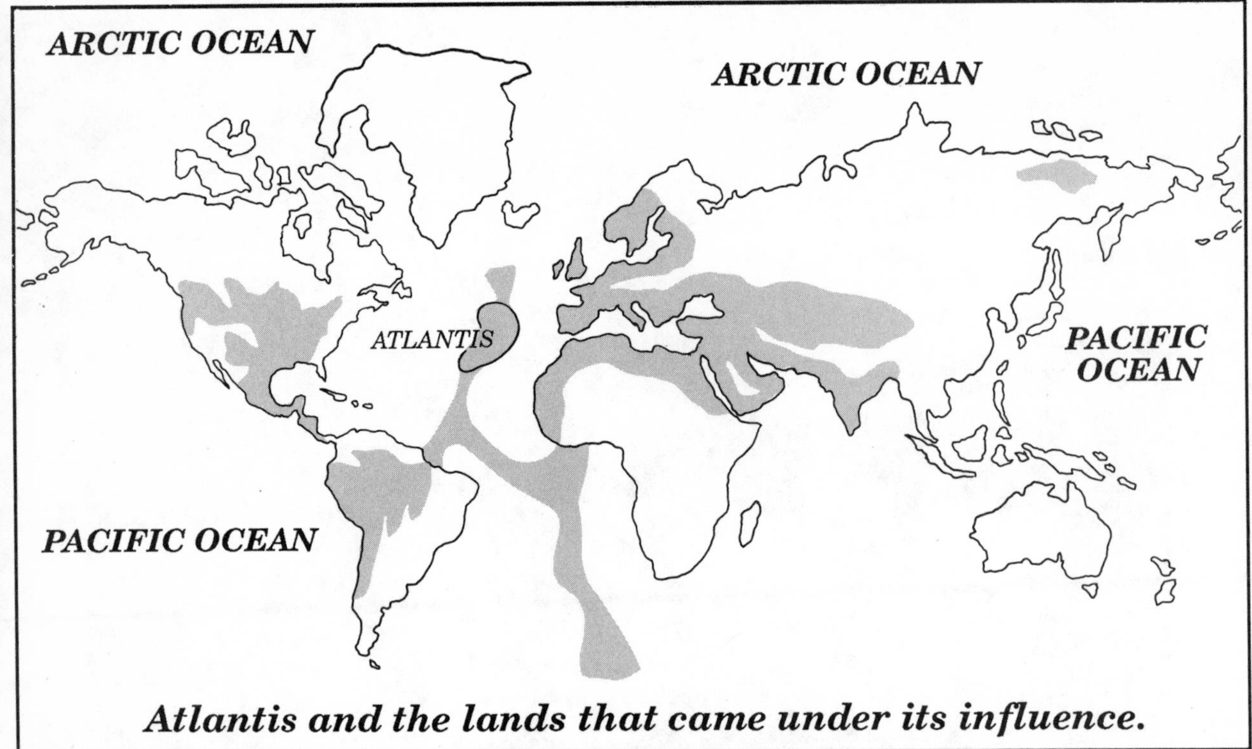

Atlantis and the lands that came under its influence.

This map shows the areas of the world Ignatius Donnelly believed were influenced by Atlantean culture.

obelisks, and *stelae* (inscribed stone monuments) are prevalent in both places. Could Atlantean travelers and, later, Atlantean survivors and their descendants have brought the advanced knowledge of Atlantis to the Americas and to Egypt?

Author Brad Steiger writes about the supernatural and the unexplained mysteries of the world. He says that the culture of Tiahuanaco, Bolivia, and that of Egypt had many similarities. Tiahuanaco's house of worship is almost a scale model of Egypt's temple of Karnak. The stones are fitted, joined, and polished in the same manner. Don't forget, also, that explorer David Zink remarked on the tight fit of the stones in the underwater ruins at Bimini. Did master builders from a common culture construct these buildings or did they teach others how to build these great monuments?

In the Andes Mountains in Bolivia, 13,000 feet above sea level, is the ancient city of Tiahuanaco. It lies in ruins. Only its huge walls and statues remain. Perhaps this is evidence of an ancient and alien race. Those who accept the existence of Atlantis believe it is the oldest city in the world, and that it was actually a part of the island of Atlantis.

In the language of the ancient Incas, "Tiahuanaco" means "Seat of the Mighty Ancients." When the Spaniards reached this city in the 1500s, it had already been long abandoned. Even the oldest living Incans did not know who had built the city. According to their legend, Tiahuanaco was built by giant gods when "the mountains were hills and the deserts were green." Who were these giant gods? Were they from Atlantis?

The legend is puzzling because geologists have said that it is impossible that the city could have been built when the mountains were hills. It would take at least hundreds of thousands of years for the mountains to be made. Yet there is some evidence that the city may have been built before the Andes reached their present height. Could they have risen thousands of feet in a short time?

Lake Titicaca, the largest lake in South America, is ten miles from Tiahuanaco. it is known as "the washbasin of the gods." In the middle of this vast lake is Sun Island. The ruins of a stone temple remain there. The city of Tiahuanaco may have been a port on the lake thousands of years ago.

According to archaeologist Arthur Posnansky, Tiahuanaco was a thriving seaport in 14,000 BC. Posnansky became devoted to this ancient city and spent thirty years studying it. He concluded that the Sun Temple was a clock based on the movement of the stars. According to studies done at Potsdam University, it was oriented to a star that was the pole star in 9550 BC. But the temple was never finished. It was suddenly and unexplainedly abandoned.

Underwater explorer Jacques Cousteau has discovered a wall of gigantic stones and evidence of

Jacques Cousteau, underwater explorer, who has attempted to find evidence of the existence of Atlantis.

''If Atlantis had not existed there would be no way of explaining the origins of the Mayan civilization.''

Scientist Otto Muck, *The Secret of Atlantis*

''Those who argue that the Mayas must have obtained their culture from elsewhere, for instance from Atlantis. . . . concentrate upon likenesses and ignore differences, which are so profound as to make the resemblances look petty and accidental.''

Author L. Sprague de Camp, *Lost Continents*

large canals on the bottom of Lake Titicaca. (Remember, there were also giant stone ruins in the waters off Bimini.) Fossils of saltwater creatures were also found in the lake, and fossilized saltwater plants were discovered in the surrounding mountains. This may mean that Tiahuanaco and Titicaca were once at sea level, possibly part of a sea gulf.

The mountains of Antarctica are part of the same range as the Andes. Was it the Atlanteans living in Tiahuanaco who mapped the Antarctic before it froze over? According to some theories about Atlantis, records and ruins of an Atlantean civilization are buried beneath the ice of Antarctica.

The Mayans

In the late 1800s, the attention of Atlantis-seekers focused on the Yucatan Peninsula of Mexico, Honduras, and Guatemala. Hidden deep within the jungles were the remains of the once mighty Mayan Empire. The age of the ruins has been estimated at between 2,000 and 4,500 years old. The estimates are based on current belief about the development of civilization and on carbon dating of objects found in and near the large stone structures. (Carbon dating involves measuring the radioactivity of the carbon atoms in an object. The radioactivity decreases at a specific rate, so the amount that is left can tell the approximate age of the object.)

Unfortunately, the stone structures, which do not contain carbon, do not respond to carbon dating methods. Some people suggest that the ruins are much older than 4,000 years and could have belonged to a very old culture—perhaps Atlantis.

The Mayans, or perhaps other cultures before them, left thousands of pyramids and stelae. The Sun Pyramid at Teotihuacan, Mexico was used to mark the sun's seasonal positions. The Great Pyramid of Cheops in Egypt also marked these solar positions, as did the temple at Tiahuanaco in Bolivia.

The stelae in Guatemala were used to measure the size of the Earth, and to map the planet. The obelisks of Egypt were also used for this purpose. John Michell, author of *The New View Over Atlantis*, wrote that the Mayan Sun Pyramid and the Great Pyramid of Cheops were part of a worldwide power system laid out across the globe by an ancient people. He believes that the system tapped the strong magnetic power of the Earth. Who set up this system? Could it have been the migrating Atlanteans?

The Mayan Empire became a popular area for explorers during the late 1800s and early 1900s. Between 1910 and 1930, engineer William Niven claimed to have found ancient ruins of whole prehistoric cities at a depth of thirty feet near Mexico City. Because of the layers of boulders and sand and pebbles, it seemed to Niven that the buildings had been struck by a series of tidal waves. Because of their depth, he estimated that the ruins were about 50,000 years old.

Many other Mayan and other ancient sites were explored. They included the city of Teotihuacan, also near Mexico City; a 230-foot-high pyramid at Tikal in Guatemala; and the city of Chichen-Itza in the northern Yucatan.

Mayan Ruins

Most of the Mayan ruins remain covered, overgrown, or ignored. But we do know that their buildings and sculptures all reflect an obsession with time. Everything the Mayans built has reference to time in relation to their own civilization.

C.W. Ceram, in his book, *Gods, Graves and Scholars*, writes, "Every Mayan construction was part of a great calendar in stone. There was no such thing as random arrangement; the Mayan aesthetic [sense of beauty] had a mathematical basis."

The Mayans had a very accurate calendar. They calculated the year at 365.24219 days. By our modern techniques, the year has been calculated at 365.242127

Were artifacts such as these stelae from two very different and geographically distant cultures influenced by descendants of Atlantis?

Two majestic pyramids—one Mayan (left), one Egyptian (right). Did Atlanteans teach the peoples of both cultures how to build them?

days. The Mayans also invented the concept of, and symbol for, zero.

The Mayans' knowledge of the stars and the universe was vast. Augustus Le Plongeon, a medical doctor and explorer in the 1800s, concluded from his investigation of Mayan ruins that the Mayans were expert mathematicians, astronomers, and navigators. He believed that they were able to compute the size of the world and the distance from the North Pole to the South Pole. He also believed that the Mayans, like the Egyptians, built their religious ideas and their beliefs about the universe into their architecture, especially their pyramids. Was it merely coincidence that several of the ancient cultures developed sophisticated mathematical concepts at about the same time?

The Mayans are a mystery. Most of their

writings—their history and the key to their hieroglyphics—were burned in the 1500s by the Catholic missionaries. They wished to wipe out all traces of the "pagan" religion. But two important documents have survived—the *Chilam Balam* and the *Popul Voh*. Both tell of a Great Flood and massive destruction. They also tell of a people coming to the Yucatan from the East.

Those who believe in the existence of Atlantis speculate that the Mayans were the descendants of the Atlanteans and that their knowledge of astronomy and mathematics was part of their ancient legacy from Atlantis.

Egypt

Egypt may also have been heavily influenced by Atlantean culture before the destruction of Atlantis.

"All along the Atlantic Littoral—on both sides of the ocean—tribes and nations could not forget [Atlantis's] existence or its fate. . . . The memory of Atlantis is recalled by massive and unexplained ruins on both sides of the Atlantic."

Author Charles Berlitz, *Atlantis, the Eighth Continent*

"Arguments of Atlantis theorists to prove the Atlantic origin of civilization from cultural similarities between various peoples are quite useless. These arguments are based on mistaken ideas of archaeology, anthropology, mythology, linguistics and associated sciences. They contain no merit."

Author Bill S. Ballinger, *Lost City of Stone*

Consider, for instance, the Great Pyramid of Cheops. It is one of the Seven Wonders of the World. It is a monument to the genius of the Egyptians in both mathematics and the measurement and study of the stars. How did the Egyptians come by this great knowledge in ancient days? Is it a coincidence that the peoples of the Americas also used their buildings for the purposes of astronomy and mathematics? Or did the Atlanteans teach both peoples?

The Great Pyramid is a mathematical marvel. According to some authorities, every measurement on the Great Pyramid is significant: The structure incorporates the value of *pi* to a precise degree. The sum of the lengths of its base sides is equal to the number of days in a year. The estimated weight of the earth can be derived by multiplying the height of the pyramid by one billion. And the estimated distance from the earth to the sun can be calculated by multiplying the height of the pyramid by ten billion. The measurements of the sides also reflect a knowledge of latitude and longitude. These concepts had supposedly not been invented when the pyramid was built.

The Great Pyramid is also closely aligned with the North Pole. And some scientists claim that flowing through the pyramid is a mysterious energy that does not fit our laws of science. Was this structure built by the genius of Atlantis? Did the Atlanteans flee to Egypt, as Edgar Cayce claimed?

Egyptian Civilization

Egypt seemed to pass from a relatively primitive period into a well-organized kingdom very suddenly. Most historians date that change at between 4000 and 3000 BC. Yet some traditions date the Great Pyramid to before the Flood. Although many authorities do not agree with this, there is some evidence to support it: Shells and fossils and a salt deposit have been found near this structure. Since the Pyramid sits in the midst of a great desert, this seems highly unusual.

According the Charles Berlitz, cultures with irrigation and pyramids developed, geographically, along a fairly straight line—at about thirty degrees north latitude. Central America, North Africa, Egypt, the Fertile Crescent of the Middle East, Iran, and India all lie along this line. If we see this path beginning in Central America and traveling east through these regions to India, there is a noticeable "break" at the Atlantic Ocean. Perhaps there was once another land there.

There Are Few Similarities, the Critics Say

Not everyone agrees with those who claim there are similarities between Egypt and the Americas. For example, L. Sprague de Camp, author of *Lost Continents*, lists the many items that Egypt and other "Old World" cultures had that the Mayans of the "New World" lacked. He asks how two civilizations founded by the same motherland could be so different!

The Mayans lacked the plow and the wheel. Although they had some food plants in common, the staple of the Egyptians was wheat while the staple of the Mayans was maize (corn). Their calendars were also very different, de Camp says. The Egyptian calendar was based on a year of twelve months having twenty-eight days each. The Mayan calendar, on the other hand, was based on a year of eighteen months having twenty days each. But both built an adjustment for leap years into their calendars. As for the hieroglyphics found in Egypt and America, de Camp says that only the principle is the same; there is no resemblance between the language or the symbols.

Megaliths and Atlantis

Megaliths are giant building stones most commonly found in countries bordering the Atlantic Ocean. Their builders, dates of origin, and purpose are undetermined. Students of Atlantis speculate about the megaliths' relationship to Atlantis.

Author L. Sprague de Camp, who believes that most of what we "know" about Atlantis is fantasy, not fact.

Mayan (above) and Egyptian (opposite page) hieroglyphs. Both are languages written with pictures (pictographs), but they are very different in style. Is it likely that they both came from the same originators?

Megalithic ruins can be simple stone monuments or large constructions having many of these great stones. Probably the most famous megalithic ruin is Stonehenge in England. In Mexico and Honduras, the Mayan ruins are often considered megalithic. Tiahuanaco, Bolivia, is a city of giant stones. In Egypt, the pyramids might be considered megalithic structures, too. There is even a megalithic site in New Hampshire called *Mystery Hill*. The great mounds built by certain Native American tribes, especially along the Mississippi Valley, are also considered megalithic.

Archaeologist Manson Valentine and explorer David Zink claim that the ruins in the waters off Bimini are megalithic. The Bimini ruins, like others in South and Central America, show great mastery of stoneworking. The blocks fit so tightly that even a knife blade cannot be inserted between them. John Michell, author of *The New View Over Atlantis*, suggests that the megalith builders originated in Atlantis. They then migrated east and west.

Megalithic markers are still being discovered. They seem to form a network based on sophisticated measurements of the movements of the sun and moon. Markers found so far seem to follow *leys*, invisible power lines, across the globe. Temples and monuments such as Stonehenge may have been built to harness or focus energy at the points where these leys intersect.

According to explorer Zink, Bimini was a site of great magnetic power and alignment with the sun and stars. It was probably a central point in the Earth's power system. Isn't it likely that the discoverers or keepers of that system would live at one of its most powerful points? And Bimini, as we have said, is often associated with Atlantis.

Modern scientists have wondered how primitive peoples were able to move the large stones into place. Michell suggests that the huge stones may have been

moved by a kind of force that modern humans no longer know about. It may be that this force could be activated only when certain magnetic and gravitational conditions existed.

John Michell believes that ancient people had a high level of knowledge concerning the elements of nature and how to use those elements for energy, measuring, and mathematical calculation. He says that this idea, however, is very difficult for some people to accept because it means that ancient peoples may have had scientific knowledge equal or even superior to our own.

The megaliths are a great mystery in themselves. But they may also be real evidence that a highly advanced culture such as Atlantis did indeed exist thousands of years before our history began.

Six

Common Legends

There is no hard evidence to prove Atlantis did or did not exist. But myths and legends from around the world help keep the debate alive. Myths and legends are stories handed down from generation to generation. They deal with gods and goddesses, heroes, nature, and human customs. They may be based on actual persons and events in the distant past, but no one knows for sure.

The Garden of Eden

Cultures around the world have legends about a time when the world was peaceful and perfect. People lived in harmony with each other and with nature. But then people lost the bliss of Paradise through their own faults and weaknesses.

In the Judeo-Christian culture of the West, the idea of Paradise is represented by the story of the Garden of Eden and Adam and Eve, the first Man and Woman, who lived there. Was Atlantis the Garden of Eden and the basis for these Paradise legends? Or do the legends simply represent our natural yearning for a perfect world? Is the idea of Eden just an invention—or an ancient memory?

A fifteenth-century Italian woodcut showing God created Eve from Adam in the Garden of Eden. Some people think Atlantis was the real Garden of Eden.

Ignatius Donnelly, author of the first modern "authoritative" book on Atlantis. While much of what he wrote about the Lost Continent is known today to be untrue, some of his ideas continue to influence Atlantists.

In his book, *Atlantis: The Antediluvian World*, Ignatius Donnelly called Atlantis the "true Antediluvian [pre-Flood] world: the Garden of Eden . . . representing a universal memory of a great land, where early mankind dwelt for ages in peace and happiness." Donnelly ardently believed in the existence of Atlantis. His research was intended to prove scientifically that Atlantis was now resting on the floor of the Atlantic Ocean.

Donnelly's pursuit of the truth about Atlantis rekindled interest in Atlantis in the late 1800s. He studied Atlantis from many angles—language, zoology, botany, history, and geology. In light of present-day understanding and information, his research is considered flawed. For example, critics point to his outdated mode of scientific reasoning. But Donnelly's book is still considered the "Bible of Modern-Day Atlantology."

According to Donnelly, Atlantis was the home of a superior race of people that lived in peace and prosperity. Civilization spread from Atlantis to the rest of the world. The descendants of the Atlanteans retained a distant memory of those ideal times in Atlantis. Donnelly suggested that Atlantis was really the basis for the later idea of Heaven and the gods. As the story was passed along, however, the home of these perfect people was moved from an island in the ocean upwards to "Heaven."

Hopi Legends

According to legends of the Hopi people of Arizona, there were several destructions of the world because the people became greedy and materialistic.

Frank Waters, in *The Book of the Hopi*, tells the story of the destruction of the "third world." (Two other worlds were destroyed before that.) According to Hopi legend, the third world was heavily populated. There were large cities and nations. People even had aircraft that they used in warfare. The people became

increasingly wicked and corrupt. A great flood destroyed this third world. Continents sank and the land and the sea changed places. Some people saved themselves by sailing from island to island until they came to a great land where they finally settled.

Both Plato and modern psychic Edgar Cayce also mention the moral corruption of the Atlanteans prior to the destruction. The Hopi believe that the "fourth world," our world, will also end because of human weakness. Is this also what Edgar Cayce warns about? Is Atlantis being recreated in our modern world?

The Flood story is found in most of the world's older cultures. This drawing is based on a Mayan wall carving. Are these flood stories based on one great flood that inundated the world—and destroyed Atlantis? Or is the story universal merely because floods are a common destructive occurrence in many parts of the world?

Mescalero Apache Legends

The Mescalero Apaches, another Native American tribe of the southwest United States, have

> ''Most scholars agree that the Indians came into the Western Hemisphere from Asia via the Bering Strait in the series of migrations.''
>
> *The New Columbia Encyclopedia*

> ''Among North American Indians there is a widespread tradition of an eastern origin with arrival by the sea.''
>
> Author Vincent H. Gaddis, *American Indian Myths and Mysteries*

legends about their ancestors that are remarkable because of their apparent connection with Atlantis, Tiahuanaco, and ancient Egypt.

According to Apache legend, Ammon-Ra was the ruler of the Men-of-the-Mountains. He originally came from the East. Because of the Great Flood, he and his people fled to the mountains from the Fire Land in the Sunrise Sea (the Atlantic Ocean). He went south to build cities of great stones in the mountains.

Ammon-Ra is also the name of the chief god of ancient Egypt. And remember the various megalithic sites in Central and South America—buildings made of great stones. Is this just coincidence? It seems very unlikely. And there are even more similarities.

The Mescalero Apaches have a fire ritual called the *Crown Dance*, in which men of the tribe wear the costumes of the ancestral Men-of-the-Mountains. They dance and chant throughout the night. The dancers wear elaborate headdresses shaped like tridents (three-pronged pitchforks) and carry spears adorned with the images of snakes. These costumes are almost identical to that worn by ancient Egypt's ram-headed god, Ammon-Ra, as he is depicted in temple wall paintings there. How can it be that peoples on both sides of the Atlantic worshipped such similar gods, gods with the same name?

There is more to consider. Atlantis was ''the Land of the Trident,'' according to tradition. The Crown of the Trident was the symbol of the royal house of Atlantis. The trident is also the symbol of Poseidon, god of the sea, in Greek mythology. According to Plato, Poseidon was the founder of Atlantis and the father of its ruler, Atlas, for whom Atlantis is named. Also, there is a 300-foot trident carved on a rocky slope in Peru in South America. The trident is recognizable only from the air and is pointing inland. It seems to be directing travelers to Tiahuanaco in Bolivia.

Lucy Taylor Hansen, an avid student of Native

American legends, showed an Apache shaman (medicine man) a photo of the gate of the ancient city of Tiahuanaco. The shaman knew the "secret sign of recognition" that the god on the gate was signaling. It was the sign of the shaman's tribe as well!

Hansen also observed that the symbols on the shaman's costume were respresentative of the Venus calendar of the ancient Mayans. Some scholars believe that the Venus calendar was inherited from a motherland long lost in ancient times. Are the Apaches the descendants of the people of Tiahuanaco and thus descendants of Atlantis as well?

According to the tribe's tradition, their ancestors once lived far to the south. They had built cities with huge stones. One such city was located in the mountains, on a lake. There were also great caves and tunnels beneath the city. This description is remarkably similar to Tiahuanaco.

Like the Hopi's ancestors, the Apaches believe their ancestors came from a land in the sea that had been destroyed by a flood. Furthermore, the Mayan

Poseidon, god of the sea, carrying his trademark trident.

Mescalaro Apache "mountain spirit" or "devil" dance. Note the trident headdresses.

book, *Chilam Balam*, tells of the destruction of the ancestral homeland and the flight of the survivors to Central and South America.

Could the Native Americans of North America be the descendants of the people of Central and South America? This contradicts the most widely-accepted theory about the migration of people to the Americas. This theory states that people came to America from the North. They crossed the Bering Strait from Asia when there was still a land bridge connecting the two continents. This occurred before the last Ice Age ended and flooded the land between Asia and North America. Over the course of thousands of years, people made their way from North America into Central, then South America.

But archaeologist Jeff Goodman asks if it isn't strange that there is no myth or legend in any of the Native American traditions that tells of a migration over land. Instead, their legends tell of their ancestors' homelands across the ocean. The best scientific evidence backs up the Bering Strait theory. Scientists say that there is no evidence to back up the Atlantic Ocean migration theory. But why, then, are there no legends to back up the scientific evidence?

"Dare we believe that the legends and myths of our ancestors are based on fact? If so, we may discover that humanity's history is in dire need of revision. Ancient manuscripts are crammed with numerous accounts of sky discs, flying chariots, cloud ships, and aerial demons."

Author Brad Steiger, *Atlantis Rising*

What Does It All Mean?

The legends and traditions of peoples around the world seem to point to an ancient, highly developed world that was destroyed before our prehistoric period even began. But our scientific data and theories do not support these legends. So what, then, *is* the truth about Atlantis?

"Pseudo-scientists such as most Atlantists assure us that all myths are founded upon fact, and then exaggerate the realistic or historical elements in them in order to support their own theories of jack-in-the-box continents."

Author L. Sprague de Camp, *Lost Continents*

Seven

The Destruction of Atlantis

If Atlantis did really exist, what could have caused this great island to disappear so completely that no certain evidence of its existence has yet been found? There are almost as many theories about the cause of Atlantis's destruction as there are about its existence.

Destruction by the Great Flood

The destruction of Atlantis, according to Ignatius Donnelly, was the basis for the Great Flood described in the Bible and other ancient literature. Cultures all around the world have legends of a great flood that wiped out almost all of the civilized world. Did such a flood engulf the entire earth and wipe out a huge portion of the population? Or was the destruction of Atlantis the basis for the legends?

Plato wrote in the *Timaeus* dialogue that Atlantis disappeared into the sea in one night and one day. Edgar Cayce, on the other hand, told of three destructions, thousands of years apart, which finally caused the whole of Atlantis to sink beneath the sea. Could these destructions have been the result of an incredible flood which survivors later described to the peo-

Old Bible woodcut of Noah's flood.

"Afterward there occurred violent earthquakes and floods, and in a single day and night of rain all your warlike men in a body sank into the earth and the island of Atlantis in like manner disappeared and was sunk beneath the sea."

Plato, *Timaeus*

"What easier way is there—in fiction, though not in fact—to destroy an island than to plunge it beneath the waves?"

Geologist Dorothy Vitaliano, quoted in *Atlantis: Fact or Fiction?*

ple in their new homeland?

Geologist Dorothy Vitaliano does not think so. She does not believe the destruction of Atlantis inspired the flood legends of so many cultures. It is highly unlikely, she says, that one huge flood washed over so many lands at once, or that only one flood is responsible for all the legends. Most ancient cultures, she reminds us, lived in great river valleys, for they were the most fertile areas. Rivers also provided food, water, and good transportation. Flooding was, and still is, quite common along these rivers. Vitaliano believes the flood legends are based on local floods that periodically have wiped out populations dwelling in the great river valleys.

The End of the Ice Age

Another natural cause of a great flood, and the destruction of Atlantis, might have been a sudden rise in sea level. Before the melting of the glaciers, sea level all over the world was about 300 feet lower than it is today. Did the melting of the glaciers at the end of the Ice Age sink Atlantis? The Ice Age ended between 11,000 and 12,000 years ago—just about the time, according to Plato, that Atlantis slipped into the sea.

But conventional geology says that the glacial melting was due to gradual temperature changes on earth. So the rise in sea level was very gradual too. At most, it may have risen only a few feet a year. That would make it impossible for glacial waters to have flooded Atlantis in a day and a night.

Geologists are not sure, however, what caused the glaciers to melt. Their best guess is that the melting was a gradual process. But what if something cataclysmic set off the glacial melting? What if a great meteor had struck the earth? Or what if the planet Venus, or a comet, had passed dangerously close to earth? What if the earth had shifted on its axis? Or again, what if ancient people set off an explosion of even greater intensity than that of today's atomic bombs? Could any of these events have caused a very quick meltdown of the glaciers? Perhaps the great island nation of Atlantis was destroyed by a tidal wave of glacial water.

Destruction by Comet or Meteor

Ignatius Donnelly devoted an entire book to the idea that Atlantis was destroyed by a collision with a comet. He also wrote that the entire earth was plunged into a period of darkness when it passed through the tail of a comet. Current research into the composition of comets, however, has eliminated this as a likelihood.

Physicist Otto Muck, a rocket researcher, wrote in *The Secret of Atlantis*, that Atlantis was destroyed by a giant meteor. According to his research, on June 5, 8498 BC, "Asteroid A did wildly go off course, break in pieces, plunge into the Atlantic's Bermuda Triangle . . . dragging with it . . . an entire island civilization." The meteor fell into the southwest part of the North Atlantic, he says, striking with the force of 30,000 H-bombs. It crushed Atlantis and unleashed a tidal wave of explosions, floods, and changes on the ocean floor. The fact that it hit at the weak point where three tectonic plates come together made it all the more devastating.

Muck also proposed that the collision, and the sinking of the large land mass, set off a chain reaction of earthquakes and tidal waves around the world. Like Donnelly, Muck believed that the sinking of Atlantis was the basis for the legends of the Great Flood.

Near-Collision with Venus

Scientist Immanuel Velikovsky turned the scientific world upside-down in the 1950s when he wrote that the planet Venus had nearly collided with Earth several times in ancient history. Venus passed so close to Earth that the Earth shook on its axis. The seasons

Comet Kohoutek. Some authorities think that Atlantis may have been destroyed by an asteroid or a comet.

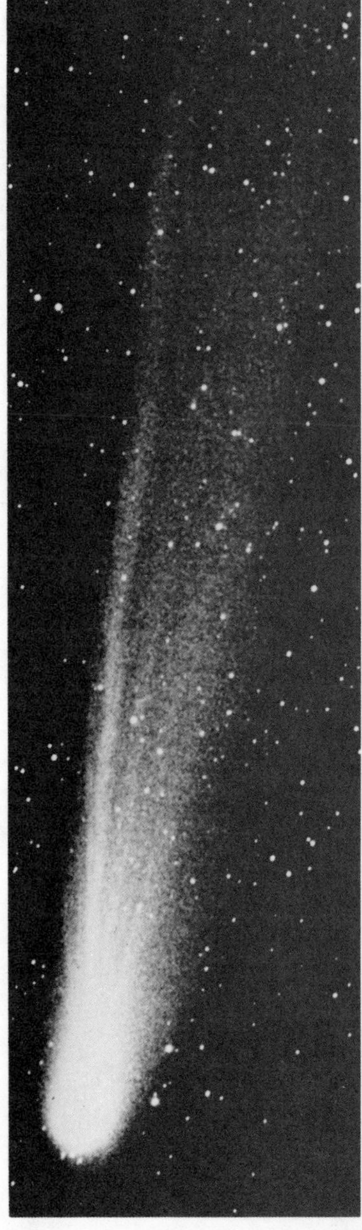

Though it looks like a picture from an old science fiction movie, this photo shows a real "death ray." Taken in 1924, this picture shows F. Grindell Matthew's machine designed to locate and destroy enemy aircraft. Might such a machine have backfired and destroyed Atlantis?

were thrown out of sequence. There were periods of great darkness. There were great changes on the surface of the planet and beneath it. Deep cracks were even created in the tectonic plates beneath the continents. If all this did occur, is it any wonder that land masses disappeared in a day and a night?

Destruction by Human Technology

Many believe that the Atlanteans caused their own destruction. Edgar Cayce claimed that the instrument of their doom was a machine capable of harnessing natural forces, perhaps a machine that could make use of the magnetic forces in rocks and crystals.

Literature of ancient India tells of aircraft, rockets, and bombs of atomic magnitude. This suggests that thousands of years ago such weapons were not only imaginable, but perhaps a reality. This literature also contains reference to atomic and molecular theory—relatively recent developments for us.

An archaeological dig in Iraq in 1947 unearthed a level of fused glass. The fused glass was similar to the fused glass created on the desert of New Mexico when the first atomic bomb was tested there.

Charles Berlitz writes in *Atlantis, the Eighth Continent*: "The concept of the Earth, in its past history, having been damaged by nuclear warfare violent enough to have modified the climate, melted the glaciers, or affected its movement on its axis and caused, in the words of the legends, 'land and water to have changed their places,' would seem to belong to the domain of science fiction." Yet he adds that science fiction and scientific fact have become rather close in recent history.

Did Atlantis destroy itself with a powerful weapon? Could a weapon have existed that is beyond even our imagination—a weapon that could evaporate an entire continent, or cause it to sink without a trace? But then who would have thought, a hundred years ago, that we would be able to create bombs that kill people but leave buildings intact (namely, the neutron bomb); or that we would have the weaponry to destroy our whole planet many times over?

"It was apparently a surge, which brought ice to lower latitudes and caused rapid melting. . . . We submit that this event, in spite of its great antiquity in cultural terms, could be an explanation for the deluge stories common to many Eurasian, Australasian and American traditions."

Oceanographer Cesare Emiliani, quoted in *The Mysterious World*

Destruction from Above

Both Plato and Edgar Cayce tell about an Atlantis in which the people had become corrupt and indirectly brought about their own destruction. Plato's story ends abruptly, just as Zeus is calling together the other Greek gods to decide how to punish Atlantis for its wickedness. Did supernatural forces—the gods—destroy Atlantis?

A psychic on David Zink's expedition links Bimini and Atlantis with space travelers from the Pleiades (the Pleiades is a group of several hundred stars in the constellation Taurus). The psychic says that these space people brought their superior scientific knowledge to Atlantis. If they could bring civilization to Atlantis, could they also destroy the civilization they helped create?

Writer J. Countryman suggests the destruction of

"Not only are those changes [at the end of the Ice Age] far too slow to have provoked traditions of catastrophe, but in any case they fell far short of being the kind of deep flood envisioned in most of the traditions."

Geologist Dorothy Vitaliano, quoted in *The Mysterious World*

Atlantis was a punishment dealt out by the ancient astronauts from the Pleiades. He maintains that the Greek gods were not immortals, but Pleiadians. Zeus was their leader. When Zeus called together the "gods" at the end of Plato's *Timaeus* dialogue, he was really calling together representatives from space to ponder the fate of the wayward Atlanteans.

The Bermuda Triangle: Key to Atlantis?

Author Charles Berlitz says that the Bermuda Triangle may hold the key to the existence and destruction of Atlantis. The Bermuda Triangle is the area in the North Atlantic where so many ships and airplanes have disappeared or experienced mysterious occurrences. Edgar Cayce believed that this is where the Atlanteans' power source is buried. Is it possible that power still radiates from this mechanism, causing the mysterious episodes in the Bermuda Triangle?

According to Berlitz, diver Ray Brown retrieved

Might a sophisticated space machine such as the one below have come from the Pleiades (right) to decide the fate of Atlantis?

a crystal from the waters of the Bermuda Triangle in 1970. Brown claims that the crystal was housed in an underwater pyramid surrounded by other ruins. Did Brown discover one of the power plants of Atlantis?

Cayce said that the Atlanteans used crystals as a source of communication and power, and ultimately, of destruction. Crystals have been used in our own day for building radios. More and more people today are returning to an old belief that crystals and other minerals have a special power that can be used for physical and spiritual healing.

Some crystal-using healers write that the Atlanteans "programmed" certain clear quartz crystals with information about Atlantis before it was completely destroyed. These healers say that, like our computer chips, crystals can contain vast amounts of information in a very tiny piece. These "programmed" crystals can be identified, they say, by a perfect triangle engraved on one of the facets of the crystal. The information can be understood by a person who meditates with the crystal and who is ready to receive such information.

Does all of this sound outrageous to you? Or is it within the realm of possibility? If we can conceive it, isn't it possible? For that matter, isn't the notion of computer chips kind of outrageous too?

Conclusion

Will We Ever Know the Truth About Atlantis?

Hundreds of books and articles have already been written about Atlantis. They have located Atlantis in Antarctica, North Africa, Sri Lanka, South Africa, France, the Arctic, Brazil, the Netherlands, the South Pacific, Central America, Spain, Iceland, Iraq, Sweden, Palestine, the Atlantic Ocean, Crete, and in the world of fantasy. Attention has focused most intensely on Crete and the Atlantic Ocean. For some people, Crete matches the description. But for many, Atlantis could only have been in the Atlantic Ocean, as Plato said.

Investigation into the Lost Continent of Atlantis opens up worlds of speculation about history, geology, philology (the study of languages), archaeology, and many other disciplines. Discussion of Atlantis invites us to think about our development here on Earth, and about the dynamic processes of the planet itself. Questioning is never ending when it comes to Atlantis. Speculation about its existence and its destruction leads to some fascinating ideas about the nature of the universe.

No doubt the debate about Atlantis will continue until Atlantis rises again or someone dredges up some

A modern city on the island of Thera. Would Atlantis resemble this if it were to rise from the sea to return to its former splendor?

artifacts that undeniably prove that it existed. But even if such proof is never found, the search for it challenges our imaginations and our beliefs—and beckons us to keep growing beyond them.

Books for Further Exploration

Wendy Stein particularly recommends the following books to readers who would like to learn more about Atlantis.

Charles Berlitz, *Atlantis, The Eighth Continent*. New York: Fawcett Crest, 1984.

Marjorie Braymer, *Atlantis, The Biography of a Legend*. New York: Atheneum, 1983.

Vincent H. Gaddis, *American Indian Myths and Mysteries*. Radnor, PA: Chilton Book Company, 1977.

Jeffrey Goodman, *Psychic Archaeology, Time Machine to the Past*. New York: Berkley Publishing Corporation, 1977.

Francis Hitching, *The Mysterious World, An Atlas of the Unexplained*. New York: Holt, Rinehart and Winston, 1978.

Otto Muck, *The Secret of Atlantis*. New York: New York Times Books, 1976.

H.R. Stahel, *Atlantis Illustrated*. New York: Grosset & Dunlap, 1980.

Brad Steiger, *Atlantis Rising*. New York: Dell Publishing Co., Inc., 1973.

Peter Thompkins, *Mysteries of the Mexican Pyramids*. New York: Harper & Row Publishers, 1976.

David Zink, *The Stones of Atlantis*. Englewood Cliffs, NJ: Prentice-Hall, Inc., 1978.

Additional Bibliography

Edgar Evans Cayce, *Edgar Cayce on Atlantis*. New York: Warner Books, 1968.

C.W. Ceram, *Gods, Graves & Scholars*. New York: Vintage Books, 1979.

Jack Countryman, *Atlantis and the Seven Stars*. New York: St. Martin's Press, 1979.

L. Sprague de Camp, *Lost Continents, The Atlantis Theme in History, Science and Literature*. New York: Dover Publications, 1970.

Ignatius Donnelly, *The Antediluvian World*. San Francisco: Harper & Row Publishers, 1971.

Charles H. Hapgood, *Maps of the Ancient Sea Kings, Evidence of Advanced Civilization in the Ice Age*. London: Turnstone Books, 1979.

John Michell, *The New View over Atlantis*. San Francisco: Harper & Row Publishers, 1983.

Edwin Ramage, editor, *Atlantis: Fact or Fiction?* Bloomington, IN: Indiana University Press, 1978.

Lytle Robinson, *Edgar Cayce's Story of the Origin and Destiny of Man*. New York: Berkley Books, 1972.

Lewis Spence, *The History of Atlantis*. New York: Bell Publishing Co, 1967.

Frank Waters, *Book of the Hopi*. New York: Penguin Books, 1963.

Index

Picture Credits

From THE MYSTERIOUS WORLD: AN ATLAS OF THE UNEXPLAINED by Francis Hitching. Copyright © 1978 by Francis Hitching. Reprinted by permission of Henry Hold and Company, Inc., 9
The Bettman Archive, 10 top and bottom, 18, 23, 34, 35, 44, 66 left & right, 67 right, 71, 72 left & right, 81 top and bottom, 89, 93, 100
Reproduced from the collection of the Library of Congress, 15, 16
Mary Ahrndt, 17, 30, 33, 36, 38 (based on an illustration in *Lost Atlantis* by J.V. Luce, by permission of Thames & Hudson, London), 51, 60, 64, 78 (after Ignatius Donnelly)
Econ Verlagsgruppe, 19
From *Atlantis: The Eighth Continent* by Charles Berlitz. G.P. Putnam's Sons, New York, 1984. Reprinted with the permission of Charles Berlitz: 21 (Comissao Regional de Turismo Azores), 59 (cartography by Julius Egloff), 91 (after a photo by Dr. J. Manson Valentine)
From the collection of the Minnesota Historical Society, 26 (photo by F. Gulekunst, Philadelphia), 90 (courtesy of Library of Congress)
Courtesy of the Greek Ministry of Culture, TAP Service, 25, 31
Courtesy of the National Archives, 43, 68
Art Resource, 29 (Scala), 47 (Marburg), 67 left (C. Berkson)
Courtesy of the Greek National Tourist Organization, 37, 39
Courtesy of Dorothy B. Vitaliano, 40
AP/Wide World Photos, 48, 52, 74
Courtesy of the Minneapolis Public Library Picture Collection, 50 top, middle, bottom, 82, 86, 87, 97
Courtesy of the U.S. Department of Energy, 54 top
Photo by H.D. Miser/US Geological Survey, 54 bottom
All rights reserved, The Metropolitan Museum of Art, 55
Courtesy of General Atomics, 57
Pino Turolla, 61, 63
American Museum of Natural History, courtesy Department Library Services (Neg. No. 39604; photo by H. Millou), 70
Courtesy of the Mexican Government Tourism Office, 77
Photo courtesy of The Cousteau Society, a member-supported non-profit environmental organization, 79
From SECRETS OF THE GREAT PYRAMID by Peter Tompkins. Copyright © 1971 by Peter Tompkins. Reprinted by permission of Harper & Row, Publishers, Inc., 83
Photo by Geoffrey Patton, 85
Photo by John Candelario; courtesy Museum of New Mexico, Neg. No. 57773, 94
Courtesy National Aeronautics and Space Administration, 99, 102 left
Mount Wilson and Las Campanas Observatories, Carnegie Institution of Washington, 102 right
The Picture Cube, photo by K. Anderson, 105

About the Author

Wendy Stein, a freelance writer and editor, majored in religion and English at Trinity College, Hartford, Connecticut. She earned an M.A. in public communications from Syracuse University in New York State.

She has written and edited materials on a variety of subjects, such as health, social studies, science, history, consumer information, and driver education. Books she has written include *Settlers in America, Your Daily Paper*, and *Taking the Wheel.*

Wendy lives in Syracuse, New York, with her ancient and wise dog, Socki. Wendy has been studying and writing about the psychic and spiritual realms for several years. She also enjoys camping and canoeing, cross-country skiing, whale-watching, and an occasional risk such as rock climbing or fire-walking.